THE NATURAL AND THE SUPERNATURAL
IN THE MIDDLE AGES

How did people of the mediaeval period explain physical phenomena, such as eclipses or the distribution of land and water on the globe? What creatures did they think they might encounter: angels, devils, witches, dog-headed people? This fascinating book explores the ways in which mediaeval people categorized the world, concentrating on the division between the natural and the supernatural and showing how the idea of the supernatural came to be invented in the Middle Ages. Robert Bartlett examines how theologians and others sought to draw lines between the natural, the miraculous, the marvelous, and the monstrous and the many conceptual problems they encountered as they did so. The final chapter explores the extraordinary thought-world of Roger Bacon as a case study exemplifying these issues. By recovering the mentalities of mediaeval writers and thinkers, the book raises the critical question of how we deal with beliefs we no longer share.

Robert Bartlett is Bishop Wardlaw Professor of Mediaeval History at the University of St. Andrews. His previous publications include *The Making of Europe* (1993), *England under the Norman and Angevin Kings* (2000), and *The Hanged Man* (2004).

THE NATURAL AND THE SUPERNATURAL IN THE MIDDLE AGES

The Wiles Lectures given at the Queen's University of Belfast, 2006

ROBERT BARTLETT

University of St. Andrews

CAMBRIDGE
UNIVERSITY PRESS

CAMBRIDGE
UNIVERSITY PRESS

University Printing House, Cambridge CB2 8BS, United Kingdom

Cambridge University Press is part of the University of Cambridge.

It furthers the University's mission by disseminating knowledge in the pursuit of education, learning and research at the highest international levels of excellence.

www.cambridge.org
Information on this title: www.cambridge.org/9780521702553

First published 2008
4th printing 2011

A catalogue record for this publication is available from the British Library

Library of Congress Cataloguing in Publication data

Bartlett, Robert, 1950–
The natural and the supernatural in the Middle Ages / Robert Bartlett.
   p.   cm.
Includes bibliographical references and index.
ISBN 978-0-521-87832-6 (hardback)
ISBN 978-0-521-70255-3 (pbk.)
1. Supernatural – History.   2. Nature.   3. Religion and science.
4. Civilization, Medieval.   I. Title.
BF1411.B27   2008
113.094′0902 – dc22   2007044426

ISBN 978-0-521-87832-6 Hardback
ISBN 978-0-521-70255-3 Paperback

Contents

List of Illustrations

Preface

It is a great honour to be invited to give the Wiles lectures. They were founded by the late Janet Boyd of County Down in memory of her father, Thomas S. Wiles, and, over the last fifty years, Mrs Boyd's imaginative generosity has encouraged numerous historians to produce, first in the lecture hall and then usually in print, reflections on the historical concerns that were preoccupying them. For a Wiles lecturer-elect, it is indeed a somewhat daunting experience to come to realize how many classics of history in fact had their origins in these lectures. Amongst the previous lecturers, I would like to make a special mention of the late Rees Davies, whose 1988 lectures appeared in print, with Rees' customary promptitude, in 1990 as *Domination and Conquest: The Experience of Ireland, Scotland and Wales 1100–1300*.[1] Rees was a much-loved man as well as a deeply respected scholar, and his death in 2005 at a relatively young age was a loss to humanity as well as to scholarship.

The strenuous four days at Queen's were enlivened by the comments and companionship of a group of distinguished visitors, many staff members of Queen's, and others who attended the lectures and discussions. I am very appreciative of this.

---

[1] R. R. Davies, *Domination and Conquest: The Experience of Ireland, Scotland and Wales 1100–1300* (Cambridge, 1990).

Professor David Hayton, Head of the School of History and Anthropology, and Trevor Boyd, the son of the benefactress, and his wife watched over us with grace and courtesy.

A special debt is owed to Nora Bartlett, who provided a valuable preliminary sounding board for these lectures.

My title is fairly grandiose, and clearly these lectures do not aim at comprehensiveness but, I hope, at illuminating examples and general considerations.

The Boundaries of the Supernatural

T HE CONCEPT OF "NATURE" IS AN ANCIENT AND CEN-
tral feature of Western thinking. Whether it has exact
correlates in other civilizations is a demanding and interesting
question, which someone else can answer. In Western culture it
has been employed in a variety of ways. Sometimes it has been
used to structure large intellectual systems (natural law theory
or natural religion, for example), but at all times it permeates
discourse. For instance, in such a formative text for the Western
intellectual tradition as St Augustine's *City of God* the word
nature and its cognates occur 600 times. Obviously not each of
those occurrences bears exactly the same weight and has exactly
the same significance, and it is always important to be aware
of the many uses to which the word can be put. C. S. Lewis
dedicates fifty pages in his *Studies in Words* to the "vast semantic
growths" around the word "nature" and its equivalents "*phusis*"
and "*kind*".[1]

Most of the texts I discuss here are in Latin, the standard
language of the educated in the Middle Ages, so it is helpful for
me that *The Dictionary of Medieval Latin from British Sources*

---

[1] *Studies in Words* (Cambridge, 1960), chap. 2, pp. 24–74 (quotation at
p. 25).

now in progress, reached the letter "N" in 2002.[2] It gives ten primary meanings of *natura*, "nature", and eleven of *naturalis*, "natural", but, since each main meaning is subdivided into often quite distinct senses, there are in reality twenty-five meanings of nature and twenty-nine of natural. The word nature can be a synonym for something as grand as the whole physical creation but is also employed in the euphemistic phrase "answer a call of nature", whereas the meanings of "natural" range from "not artificially made" to "of illegitimate birth", from "normal" to "native". And this is only from British sources!

However, I am not going to pursue a doggedly definitional path. The value, for me, of the dichotomy "natural/super-natural" is that it leads directly to investigation of medieval debates, to conflicting views of what exists and different ideas of what an explanation consists of. This book is concerned with debates and differences in the medieval period – there will be nothing about "the medieval mind".

Some intellectual historians, like some literary scholars or anthropologists, seem to have a strong urge to search for the inner coherence of the beliefs of those they study and might talk easily of "belief *systems*". This urge is doubtless well intentioned but seems to prejudge the issue. What of our own beliefs? I would be surprised if a thorough and sincere review of my own beliefs concluded that they were consistent, coherent, and steady. Like most people, I think I hold many discordant beliefs. Their discord only becomes apparent, however, in certain circumstances – this, in the terms made familiar by the historian of science Thomas Kuhn, is when latent anomalies in our paradigms become visible and uncomfortable.[3] I look at several instances of such intellec-tual discomfort in the Middle Ages.

[2] Fascicule 7, prepared by D. R. Howlett (published for the British Academy by Oxford University Press).
[3] *The Structure of Scientific Revolutions* (Chicago, 1962).

In fact the concept of "nature" leads naturally to debate, for it is usually defined *against* something. The natural can be contrasted with the artificial, that is, the man-made, with grace, that is, the God-given, with the unnatural, with human society, and so on. C. S. Lewis, in the work just mentioned, actually structures much of his discussion by asking, "What is the implied opposite to nature?"[4] Any concept that is so dyadic will generate discussion about its boundaries and its contraries.

I start my enquiry with a concrete example of the discourse of the natural and supernatural from the central Middle Ages.

Like all scriptural religions, medieval Catholic Christianity gave birth to a rich culture of textual analysis, exegesis, and commentary. The Word of God was scanned, pondered, and elucidated, and then these elucidations were themselves scanned, pondered, and elucidated. The Gloss, that is, detailed commentary, was a characteristic fruit of such a process. A telling instance is provided by the layers that built up on the biblical passage Genesis 2: 21–2 (here I give the King James version):

> And the Lord God caused a deep sleep to fall upon Adam, and he slept: and he took one of his ribs, and closed up the flesh instead thereof; and the rib, which the Lord God had taken from the man, made he a woman, and brought her unto the man.

Now this remarkable passage could be the starting point for any number of reflections, not least, of course, on its deep message about the secondary nature of woman. In the schools of twelfth-century Europe, however, it provoked a different chain of thought. Around the middle of that century, in Paris, the intellectual centre of Catholic Christianity, Peter Lombard composed his *Four Books of Sentences*, a work of systematic theology which was to be a standard university text for hundreds of years

[4] *Studies in Words* (as in n. 1), p. 43.

3

to come. This passage from Genesis stimulated in his mind not thoughts about female subordination, but an austerely philosophical question:

> When God created the world, was its character such that woman *had to be* born from man's ribs or merely such that she *could be* born in that way?[5]

The ancient Middle Eastern legend of Adam and Eve, dealing with the creation of man and the creation of woman, had thus stirred the mind of this twelfth-century academic to address the profound question of necessity and contingency. It is a classic Scholastic *quaestio*: "quaeritur an ... an" – "it is asked whether A or B". "What kind of universe do we live in?" was his question. "Is everything laid down immutably, or are there undetermined potentialities?"

It is a big question, but Peter Lombard did his best to give an answer. And, for a Scholastically trained theologian of the time, the first task was obviously to distinguish different senses:

> The causes of all things are in God; but the causes of some things are in God and in creatures, the causes of some things in God alone.[6]

---

[5] Sed quaeritur an ratio quam Deus primis operibus concreavit id haberet, ut secundum ipsam ex viri latere feminam fieri necesse foret, an hoc tantum ut fieri posset: Peter Lombard, *Sententiae in IV libris distinctae* 2. 18. 5, ed. Collegium S. Bonaventurae (3rd ed., 2 vols., *Spicilegium Bonaventurianum* 4–5, Grottaferrata, 1971–81) 1, p. 418; Peter Lombard's whole discussion here is deeply dependent on that of Augustine, *De genesi ad litteram* 9. 17–18, ed. J. Zycha (Corpus Scriptorum Ecclesiasticorum Latinorum 28, 1894), pp. 290–3 (*Patrologia latina* 34: 405–8).

[6] Omnium igitur rerum causae in Deo sunt; sed quarundam causae et in Deo sunt et in creaturis, quarundam vero causae in Deo tantum sunt: *Sententiae* (as in previous note) 2. 18. 6, p. 419.

1. CREATION OF EVE. Psalter-Hours of Yolande de Soissons, Amiens, France, between 1280 and 1299. The creation of Eve from Adam's rib as described in Genesis 2 had stimulated philosophical and theological discussion since patristic times. In the twelfth century, Peter Lombard took up the theme in his *Four Books of Sentences*, which was to become the standard theology text-book of the Latin West. Peter asked, "When God created the world, was its character such that woman *had to be* born from man's ribs or merely such that she *could be* born in that way?" This, in turn, led him to a theory of nature and miracle. (The Pierpont Morgan Library, New York. MS M.729, fol. 293v.)

To clarify the first category, those things whose causes "are in God and in creatures", Peter Lombard employed St Augustine's concept of "seminal natures" or "seminal reasons":

> God has implanted "seminal natures" in things, according to which things come forth from other things, from this seed such a grain, from this tree such a fruit, etc.... they were implanted into things by God at the initial creation. And just as creatures are mutable, so too these causes can be altered; the cause which is in the immutable God, however, cannot be changed.[7]

The causes that are in God and creatures are therefore both primordial, in that they were implanted by God at the creation, and mutable, like all creatures. In contrast, the causes that are in God alone are immutable. Peter Lombard has thus moved from the Genesis verses to a theory that causes are of two different kinds (and in the Western tradition ontology, the science of being, often assumes that a key distinction is different kinds of cause). According to Peter Lombard, following Augustine, God had implanted the seminal causes in things – a horse will give birth to a horse, an apple tree bears apples – but had reserved certain things to himself alone. He believes this distinction can be expressed in the language of the natural:

> Whatever happens according to the seminal cause is said to happen naturally (*naturaliter*), for in this way the course of nature becomes known to men. Other things are beyond nature (*praeter naturam*), since their causes are in God alone.[8]

---

[7] ...inseruit Deus seminales rationes rebus, secundum quas alia ex aliis proveniunt, ut de hoc semine tale granum, de hac arbore talis fructus, et huiusmodi.... in prima rerum conditione rebus a Deo insitae sunt. Et sicut creaturae mutabiles sunt, ita et hae causae mutari possunt; quae autem in immutabili Deo causa est, non mutari potest: ibid. 2. 18. 5, p. 419.

[8] Et illa quidem quae secundum causam seminalem fiunt, dicuntur naturaliter fieri, quia ita cursus naturae hominibus innotuit; alia vero praeter naturam, quorum causae tantum sunt in Deo: ibid. 2. 18. 6, p. 419.

Here is a central dualism: the natural and what is beyond nature. As we shall see, at the time Peter Lombard was writing, in the mid-twelfth century, the word "supernatural" was scarcely known, let alone widespread, but, if it had been, he would surely have employed it to label these "things beyond nature".

Hence we see, in this influential Parisian theologian, a clear division of those things in the universe: some are natural, follow their seminal reason, are part of the course of nature known to man; others are beyond nature, and their cause is in God alone.

In subsequent centuries, the style of thinking that Peter Lombard embodied, with its careful distinctions of sense, analytical ingenuity, and the constant impulse towards abstraction, all, of course, on a bedrock of Scripture, became the dominant mode in the universities that arose in France, Italy, and elsewhere in the late twelfth and thirteenth centuries. That style is termed by historians "Scholasticism," and its most familiar representative is Thomas Aquinas. By his time, a standard rung in the theologian's ladder was the composition of a commentary on Peter Lombard's *Sentences*, and Aquinas dutifully fulfilled this requirement. His *Commentary on the Sentences*, written around 1255, naturally included discussion of the passage I have just been talking about, that is, Lombard's exposition of Genesis 2: 21–2, the creation of Eve from Adam's rib.

Aquinas was stimulated by his predecessor's analysis into outlining his own definition and classification of miracles. A miracle, he writes, is something "wonderful in itself" which he defines as follows:

> Something is "wonderful in itself" when its cause is absolutely hidden, when there is a power in the thing, which, if it followed its true nature, would produce a different result. Of this kind are the things caused directly by God's power (the most unknown cause)

7

in a way different from that exhibited by the order of natural causes. . . . [9]

So, like Peter Lombard, Aquinas is looking for definitions in terms of type of cause: some things are caused by "the most unknown cause", God's direct power, others are part of "the order of natural causes". The concept of the miraculous thus depends on the concept of the natural, and this interdependence is even more explicit in Aquinas's categorization of miracles. According to him, they fall into three categories: "above nature", "beyond nature", and "against nature". It would be a digression to explore this further here, but it is worth stressing that, for Aquinas, what determines his classification of miracles is their relationship to nature, a relationship which he couches in a semi-metaphorical language of location – above, beyond, against.

Christian definitions of miracle have tended to revolve around three central conceptions: miracles can be characterized by their causation, by the sense of wonder they arouse, or by their function as signs. Some thinkers take a strong stance on one of these

---

[9] Admirabile autem in se est id cuius causa simpliciter occulta est, ita etiam quod in re est aliqua virtus secundum rei veritatem per quam aliter debeat contingere. Hujusmodi autem sunt quae immediate a virtute divina causantur, quae est causa occultissima, alio modo quam se habeat ordo causarum naturalium: *Super Sententiis*, lib. 2 d. 18 q. 1 a. 3 co., Thomas Aquinas, *Opera omnia*, ed. Roberto Busa (7 vols., Stuttgart-Bad Cannstatt, 1980) 1, pp. 176–7. Aquinas has a succinct discussion of miracles in *Summa contra Gentiles* 3. 98–107, ibid. 2, pp. 92–5. Discussions of Aquinas' theory of miracle are often from a denominational viewpoint: Aloïs Van Hove, *La Doctrine du miracle chez saint Thomas et son accord avec les principes de la recherche scientifique* (Wetteren, 1927); Gilles Berceville, "L'Étonnante alliance: évangile et miracles selon saint Thomas d'Aquin", *Revue Thomiste* 103 (2003), pp. 5–74 (esp. pp. 19–29); François Pouliot, *La Doctrine du miracle chez Thomas d'Aquin: Deus in omnibus intime operatur* (Paris, 2005).

ideas, whereas others attempt to integrate them.[10] In general terms, the medieval Latin West inherited from Augustine a stress on the wonderfulness of miracles. They are God's work and amazing. But then again, all God's works are amazing. As Augustine put it, "the world itself is a miracle greater and more excellent than all the things that fill it".[11] It is a style of thinking that might inspire reverential awe but was unlikely to generate clear conceptual categorization of the type in which Scholastic theologians dealt. For thinkers in that tradition, such as Peter Lombard and Thomas Aquinas, the heart of a definition of miracle lay in the way that it was distinct from "the order of natural causes". Hence Scholastic theorists of miracle, in stressing the primary importance of different orders of causation, created a sharper line between miracle and nature than that inherited from the patristic tradition.[12]

In the thirteenth century, as the theologians elaborated and pondered their definitions of miracle, there arose a new and very practical need that stimulated thinking about the distinction between the supernatural and the natural. This was the canonization process. Although the cult of the saints had been part of Christianity from early in its history, the precise, legally defined

---

[10] There are some relevant general considerations in John A. Hardon, "The Concept of Miracle from St. Augustine to Modern Apologetics", *Theological Studies* 15 (1954), pp. 229–57; Richard Swinburne, *The Concept of Miracle* (London, 1970); Benedicta Ward, *Miracles and the Medieval Mind: Theory, Record and Event 1000–1215* (Aldershot and Philadelphia, 1982), chapter 1; André Vauchez, *Saints, prophètes et visionnaires: le pouvoir surnaturel au Moyen Âge* (Paris, 1999), pp. 39–55.

[11] cum sit omnibus quibus plenus est procul dubio maius et excellentius etiam ipse mundus miraculum: *De civitate dei* 21. 7, ed. B. Dombart and A. Kalb (2 vols., *Corpus Christianorum, series latina* 47–8, 1955), vol. 48, p. 768.

[12] There are some brief but pertinent observations on this contrast in Lorraine Daston, "Marvelous Facts and Miraculous Evidence in Early Modern Europe", *Critical Inquiry* 18 (1991), pp. 93–124, at pp. 95–9.

procedure that characterized papal canonization was a novelty devised around the year 1200. One of the new features of this procedure was the interrogatory. This was a set of questions, drawn up at the beginning of a canonization process, designed to channel the flood of testimony that such occasions provoked on the virtues and miracles of the candidate for sanctity.[13]

As one would expect, the existence of a fixed questionnaire guided what the witnesses in a canonization process might say. Here are some of the questions listed in the interrogatory for the canonization process of Thomas de Cantilupe, bishop of Hereford, a process which took place in 1307: witnesses were to be asked "if his miracles were above or contrary to nature"; "what words were used by those who requested that these miracles be performed"; and "if in the operation of these miracles herbs or stones were applied or any other natural or medicinal things".[14] Clearly the papal commissioners in charge of the inquest were aiming at setting certain dichotomies before those they cross-examined and those dichotomies would push witnesses to express themselves in the language of the natural and its opposites.

Some indicative examples of how this worked in practice may be cited from another canonization process, that of cardinal Peter

---

[13] The first canonization process in which such an interrogatory was used was that of St Dominic in 1233; a standard formulary for inquiring about miracles had already been devised in the preceding year: André Vauchez, *Sainthood in the Late Middle Ages* (Eng. tr., Cambridge, 1997), pp. 48–50.

[14] si dicta miracula fuerunt supra vel contra naturam . . . quibus verbis utebantur illi qui petebant dicta miracula fieri . . . si in operatione dictorum miraculorum apposite herbe vel lapides vel alique alie res naturales vel medicinales: *Inquisitio de fide, vita et moribus, fama et miraculis . . . Thome de Cantilupo*, MS Vatican City, Biblioteca Apostolica Vaticana, Vat. Lat. 4015, fol. 4v. For further discussion, see R. Bartlett, *The Hanged Man: A Story of Miracle, Memory and Colonization in the Middle Ages* (Princeton, 2004), esp. pp. 13–14, 23–4, and 110–11.

of Luxemburg, which took place in January 1390. The cardinal had died only three years earlier, in 1387, but already 180 miracles had been attributed to his intercession.[15] One of the things that the witnesses to the late cardinal's miraculous powers of healing frequently mentioned was that the cures he effected were beyond the powers of nature (the depositions were of course mostly given in the vernacular but recorded in Latin). Thus in the summer of 1387, a sergeant-of-arms of the pope was seized with vomiting and diarrhoea: "when he was visited by the doctors, it was judged, according to nature (*secundum naturam*), that it was impossible for him to escape death".[16] It was at this point that his mother invoked the aid of the recently deceased Peter. Another cure involved a man who had blinded himself accidentally with a knife, so that "it was impossible for his sight to be restored according to nature".[17] Henrietta, widow of an Avignonese notary, suffered for three months from a swollen arm. She eventually sought the help of the saint, "despairing that the arm would heal naturally (*naturaliter*)".[18]

Even more telling is a miracle involving a boy who had been standing on the bridge at Avignon (really) when a rope pulling a passing boat had accidentally caught him and dragged him off the bridge. Even though the boy could not swim and he

---

[15] *Processus de Vita et Miraculis B. Petri de Luxemburgo, Acta sanctorum,* Julii 1 (Antwerp, 1719), pp. 527–607; for the number of miracles, Vauchez, *Sainthood* (as in n. 13), p. 503. There is a good brief introduction to Peter and his cult in Richard Kieckhefer, *Unquiet Souls: Fourteenth-Century Saints and their Religious Milieu* (Chicago, 1984), pp. 33–44, 125–7.

[16] qui per medicos visitatus, judicatus fuit secundum naturam, impossibile esse ipsum evitare mortem: *Processus* (as in previous note) no. 121, col. 570.

[17] quod impossibile erat secundum naturam lumen eidem restaurari: ibid., no. 138, col. 572.

[18] de dicti brachii sanitate naturaliter recuperanda desperans: ibid., no. 164, col. 575.

was in the river for a long time – as long as it takes to say the psalm *Miserere mei* twice, according to one witness – he was not drowned and was eventually pulled out by a shipman with a gaffe (*unum baculum, sive gaf*, in the Latin). One witness to this event was asked directly "if he believed that the boy escaped naturally or miraculously (*naturaliter, vel miraculose*)?"[19] It would be hard to imagine a more striking example of a leading question. Naturally the witness replied "miraculously".

Such instances show the way that a probing investigation into the miraculous, conducted, as it was, by men with sophisticated Scholastic ideas about how the universe ran, could encourage thinking in terms of the natural.[20] An obvious twin of the natural is the supernatural, and it is unsurprising that exactly the period that sees the creation of standard questionnaires on miracles, the thirteenth century, sees also the appearance, for the first time, of the word "supernatural" (*supernaturalis*) as a significant tool for organizing thought.

The Catholic theologian Henri de Lubac traced the evolution of this term in Christian theological writings in a work published in 1946.[21] He recognized that the idea itself could be well expressed periphrastically by the phrase "above nature (*supra naturam*)", which was common from the fourth century onwards, but there

---

[19] Interrogatus si credit quod naturaliter, vel miraculose dictus puer evasit?: ibid., no. 209, col. 593; the process contains several other accounts of this miracle. For instance, the reference to the gaff and the psalm is no. 201, col. 591.

[20] For an excellent study of how a canonization process might force the witnesses to consider the "boundaries and rules by which they defined the natural and the supernatural", see Laura Smoller, "Defining the Boundaries of the Natural in Fifteenth-century Brittany: The Inquest into the Miracles of Saint Vincent Ferrer (d. 1419)", *Viator* 28 (1997), pp. 333–59 (quotation at p. 358).

[21] Henri de Lubac, *Surnaturel: études historiques* (Paris, 1946), pp. 323–428, "Aux origines du mot 'surnaturel'", esp. 369–73.

is something significant about a new coinage. Even if the mere word "supernatural" does not enable writers and thinkers to say something they could not say before, its appearance surely indicates that they wanted to say it more often and more conveniently. It is therefore important that it is in the thirteenth century that, in de Lubac's words, "*supernaturalis* will begin to be used as a common term (*un mot courant*)". He points especially to its employment by Thomas Aquinas: "after him, the distinction natural/supernatural tends to replace many analogous distinctions".[22] De Lubac's conclusions certainly seem well founded. The Index Thomisticus (which, it should be pointed out, also indexes some works not by Aquinas) gives 370 instances of the word. For example, returning to our Genesis account, Aquinas asserts that the creation of the universe in such a way that woman could be produced from the rib of man was effected "through supernatural power (*per virtutem supernaturalem*)".[23] To keep a sense of proportion, it is worth noting that the Index also lists 43,000 uses of "nature" and "natural".

Lubac's survey indicates that the term "supernatural" was rare before the twelfth century. The main exception is in the works of the unusual ninth-century scholar John the Scot, who employed it both in his own writings and in his translations from Greek, but John the Scot is an isolated case.[24] Otherwise, the new term

---

[22] Ibid., pp. 371–3, 398–9.

[23] *Super Sententiis*, lib. 2 d. 18 q. 1 a. 1 ad 5, in *Opera omnia* (as in note 9) 1, p. 176.

[24] John the Scot seems to have devised the term as a Latin equivalent for the 'ὑπερφυής of the Pseudo-Dionysius, whom he translated, and then used it extensively in his own *Periphyseon* (ed. Edouard Jeaneau, 5 vols., *Corpus Christianorum, continuatio medievalis* 161–5, 1996–2003). Denys l'Aréopagite, *La Hiérarchie céleste*, ed. and tr. Günter Heil and Maurice de Gandillac (Sources chrétiennes 58, 1958), p. 153 n. 1, lists all occurrences of 'ὑπερφυής and 'ὑπερφυῶς in the works of Pseudo-Dionysius and also argues that "merveilleux" is a better translation than "surnaturel" for the

fits well into that efflorescence of novel technical terms in philosophy and theology that characterized high Scholasticism. As Francis Bacon noted, looking back from the seventeenth century on "the schoolmen", as he called them, medieval Scholastic writers showed great "liberty to coin and frame new terms of art to express their own sense".[25]

It is, of course, always a risky business to assert this or that occurrence is the earliest use of a term. After all, it only needs one counter-example to be falsified. The new tool of machine-readable texts has made this a much less hazardous proposition, however. De Lubac wrote at a time when writing the history of terms could not be based on the swift scanning of a database but required one to read everything. He dealt mainly with theological texts. What if we turn to another kind of text which might well be thought likely to generate the language of the supernatural, namely, hagiographical writings, that is, the Lives of the saints and accounts of their miracles? Fortunately, in modern conditions, we now have a huge database that can be searched for these purposes. The Acta Sanctorum Database contains the text of the sixty-eight printed volumes of the Acta Sanctorum published by the Bollandists, a branch of the Jesuits specializing in hagiography. The Acta Sanctorum is organized not alphabetically or chronologically but calendrically, by saints' days. The Bollandists published their first two volumes, dealing with the saints whose feasts fall in the month of January, in 1643. In 1925, the series reached the saints of 10 November. There can be few if any publishing histories like it.

---

term. The two words are not uncommon in Greek patristic writers; examples are cited in *A Patristic Greek Lexicon*, ed. G. W. H. Lampe (Oxford, 1961), p. 1443 s.vv.

[25] *Advancement of Learning* (London, 1605) 1. 4. 2.

The outcome of a search on the word "supernatural (*super-naturalis*)" and its various grammatical forms in this database is as follows.[26] First, the word is not particularly common. In all the hundreds of hagiographic texts included in the Acta Sanctorum, we find fewer than fifty instances. Second, these show a clear chronological distribution: not one is earlier than the mid-thirteenth century, precisely the time when, according to de Lubac, Thomas Aquinas was bringing the word "supernatural" into common theological discourse. Third, there is a noticeable tendency for the term to be used by the mendicant friars, Franciscans and Dominicans alike. Indeed, amongst the earliest uses of "supernatural" is that by Bonaventure, writing his Life of St Francis in the early 1260s, and other early examples include Lives of St Dominic and Thomas Aquinas himself.[27] The new

[26] One should note that several of the occurrences of "supernaturalis" and its forms in the Acta Sanctorum Database and the Patrologia Latina Database turn out to be "spiritalis" or "spiritualis" when newer and better editions can be checked. Two such cases are Jocelin of Furness' *Vita Patricii*, *Acta sanctorum*, Martii 2 (Antwerp, 1668), pp. 540–80, at p. 577, where the Bollandists' "supernaturali etiam more" should be "spiritali eciam sudore" – a reading kindly supplied by Richard Sharpe from his own draft edition; and Gilbert Crispin's *Vita Herluini* (*Patrologia latina* 150, cols. 697–714, at col. 712), where "supernaturalis" should be "spiritualis", as in *The Works of Gilbert Crispin*, ed. Anna Sapir Abulafia and G. R. Evans (London, 1986), "Vita Herluini", pp. 185–212, at p. 212. In general, the effect of such corrections is to make the thirteenth-century emergence of the term even more evident.

[27] Bonaventure, *Legenda maior S. Francisci* 4 ("supernaturali virtute"), 5 ("supernaturaliter"), *Analecta Franciscana* 10 (1926–41), pp. 555–652, at pp. 573, 581; Dietrich von Apolda, *Vita S. Dominici* (of 1297) 25 ("nec naturaliter, sed supernaturaliter ac divinitus"), *Acta sanctorum*, Augusti 1 (Antwerp, 1733), pp. 562–632, at p. 612; William de Tocco, *Vita S. Thomae Aquinatis* 33 ("quod mirabiliter Deus revelaret miraculo, quod supernaturaliter concessisset ex dono"), in *Fontes Vitae S. Thomas Aquinatis*, ed. D. Prümmer and M.-H. Laurent (Documents inédits publiés par la Revue Thomiste 6 fascicules, 1912–37), pp. 57–160 (fasc. 2), at p. 107, and

Latin coinage came into the vernacular languages at the end of the Middle Ages, appearing for the first time in French in 1375 and in English around the middle of the following century, in both cases by direct modelling on the Latin word.[28]

The history of the term "supernatural" in hagiographic writing thus corresponds exceptionally well with that in general theological writing. The mendicants, high Scholasticism, and the supernatural were born together.

Clearly, one would not wish to pin too much on the history of a single term, but it does seem that a new explicitness in the categorization of phenomena marked the period from the thirteenth century on. Theologians, hagiographers, and papal commissioners in canonization proceedings were elaborating and insisting on a particular mental geography, in which

ed. Claire Le Brun-Gouanvic, *Ystoria sancti Thome de Aquino de Guillaume de Tocco* (1323). *Édition critique, introduction et notes* (Studies and Texts 127: Pontifical Institute of Medieval Studies, Toronto, 1996), p. 161.

[28] *Dictionnaire historique de la langue française*, ed. Alain Rey (2 vols., Paris, 1992) 2, p. 2055, s.v. *"surnaturel"*, records the earliest use of the vernacular *"supernaturel"* as "1375, Robert de Presles". This must refer to the translation of Augustine's *City of God* by Raoul (not Robert) de Presles, which was completed in that year. Raoul's translation work led him to create other neologisms: Olivier Bertrand, "Les néologismes religieux dans la traduction de la Cité de Dieu par Raoul de Presles ou comment christianiser le lexique latin", in *Actes du 23e Congrès International de Linguistique et de Philologie Romanes*, ed. Fernando Sanchez Miret (6 vols. in 5, Tübingen, 2003) 3, pp. 43–7. See also Charity Cannon Willard, "Raoul de Presles's Translation of Saint Augustine's *De Civitate Dei*", in *Medieval Translators and their Craft*, ed. Jeanette Beer (Kalamazoo, 1989), pp. 329–46.

The earliest instance recorded in the *Oxford English Dictionary* is from a mid-fifteenth-century translation of Thomas à Kempis' *Imitation of Christ*, where his Latin phrase *naturaliter vel supernaturaliter* is rendered "naturely or supernaturaly": *The Earliest English Translation of the First Three Books of the De imitatione Christi*, ed. John K. Ingram (Early English Text Society, extra series 63, 1893), p. 94 (numbered in this version as 3. 24, corresponding to 3. 22 of the Latin text).

events could be assigned to particular domains, this natural, that supernatural.

In the second part of this chapter, I address two large questions that arise from what I have been discussing. First, what were the chief problems over the boundaries of the supernatural, that is, when deciding what was natural and what was not, which were the fraught areas for thinkers of the medieval period? Second, and very speculatively, I want to conclude by asking how developments in discussion of the natural and supernatural fit into the general cultural and intellectual history of the high and late Middle Ages, focussing in particular on the question: Was there a contraction of the sphere of the supernatural in that period?

To turn to the first topic. We have seen the elaboration of a new term, the supernatural, the essence of which is to mark off from the natural something else. Marking off the natural from other things had always been a major concern of Western thinkers, for if nature is not to be regarded, somewhat vacuously, as a synonym for "everything", it obviously has things it is defined against. In the instances discussed so far, the important borderline has been between nature and miracle, but this was not the only problem of classification that preoccupied medieval thinkers. There were other categories that needed to be defined, both against nature and against each other. Delimiting these was a concern of any writer who had to think about the regularities of the world, and this meant not only theologians but also historians, travel writers, and others.[29]

---

[29] In an important article, Jacques Le Goff notes that "in the twelfth and thirteenth centuries supernatural phenomena were divided, in the West, into three categories, fairly clearly delineated by three adjectives: *mirabilis, magicus, miraculosus*": Jacques Le Goff, "The Marvelous in the Medieval West", in *The Medieval Imagination* (Eng. tr., Chicago, 1988), pp. 27–44, at p. 30; see also Caroline Walker Bynum, "Miracles and Marvels: The Limits of Alterity", in *Vita religiosa im Mittelalter: Festschrift für Kaspar Elm*

For instance, in a work probably completed in 1215, Gervase of Tilbury, a kind of international courtier, introduced a collection of amazing tales by making the following distinction. He starts by discussing the general category of unfamiliar and unusual things (*inaudita*, literally, "things unheard of"). These, he says, intrigue us "partly because we marvel at the alteration in the natural course of affairs, partly from our ignorance of the cause, the source of which is completely unknown to us". So there are things in the world that are not part of the ordinary course of nature and the cause of which is mysterious. Gervase then goes on to divide this general category into two:

> From these arise two things, miracles and wonders (*miracula et mirabilia*), although the end result of both is amazement. Now we commonly call things miracles that are beyond nature and that we ascribe to the divine power.... However, we call things marvels that are beyond our understanding, even when they are natural.[30]

---

zum 70. Geburtstag, ed. Franz J. Felten and Nikolas Jaspert (Berlin, 1999), pp. 799–817.

[30] Que inaudita percipiuntur amplectimur, tum ex mutatione cursus naturalis quam admiramur tum ex ignorancia cause cuius ratio nobis est imperscrutabilis.... Ex hiis, duo proueniunt: miracula et mirabilia, cum utrorumque finis sit admiratio. Porro miracula dicimus usitatius que preter naturam diuine uirtuti ascribimus.... Mirabili vero dicimus que nostre cognicioni non subiacent, etiam cum sunt naturalia...: Gervase of Tilbury, *Otia Imperialia* 3. pref., ed. S. E. Banks and J. W. Binns (Oxford, 2002), p. 558. See Michael Rothmann, "*Mirabilia vero dicimus, quae nostrae cognitioni non subiacent, etiam cum sint naturalia*. Wundergeschichten zwischen Wissen und Unterhaltung: der 'Liber de mirabilibus mundi' ('Otia Imperialia') des Gervasius von Tilbury", in *Mirakel im Mittelalter: Konzeptionen, Erscheinungsformen, Deutungen*, ed. Martin Heinzelmann, Klaus Herbers and Dieter R. Bauer (Beiträge zur Hagiographie 3, Stuttgart, 2002), pp. 399–432.

From out of the undifferentiated category of the unusual and inexplicable, Gervase has thus distinguished two subgroups, on the one hand miracles, which are beyond nature and caused by God directly, on the other hand marvels, which are natural even if inexplicable and unusual. It is fairly clear what Gervase means in practice by natural marvels from the following examples in his collection: people born with no head, bearded ladies, the power of fennel to ward off enchantment, and so forth.[31] It is the kind of miscellaneous and sensationalist assortment that might remind us of nineteenth-century fairground attractions. Gervase's mental map thus places marvels in the category "natural". Of course, they are an unusual part of nature, to be distinguished from the regular patterns, and as a consequence his nature is not uniform – it contains both regularities and anomalies.

Such distinctions are not uncommon. They served to maintain important conceptual borders, as can be seen clearly in the comments Thomas Aquinas makes on monsters. This forms part of his discussion of the creation of Eve already mentioned. "Monsters occur in nature", he writes, and then makes a distinction: "they occur beyond the intention of active nature but they are not termed miracles."[32] His phrasing, "in nature" yet "beyond the intention of active nature" secures for the monstrous a special place in the natural world and yet keeps the category "miracle" intact for what he wants to use it for. Because Aquinas thought it important not to conflate the miraculous and the monstrous, he preserved the distinction by consigning monsters to nature, where they shared a home with natural marvels.

---

[31] Gervase, *Otia* (as in previous note) 3. 75, 76, 83, pp. 700, 712–14.

[32] monstra in natura contingunt, et praeter intentionem naturae agentis; non tamen miracula dicuntur: *Super Sententiis*, lib. 2 d. 18 q. 1 a. 3 arg. 6, *Opera omnia* (as in note 9), 1, p. 176.

Another important distinction that it was crucial to maintain was that between miracle and magic. Again, Aquinas provides a succinct illustration. "God alone can perform miracles", he writes, and "true miracles are requested by someone from God". The miracles of the saints would obviously be of this type. If this is not the case, however, and "it appears that a creature is performing miracles, then they are not true miracles." He then goes on to explain how such apparent miracles are performed: "they are performed through some forces of natural things, although hidden from us, such as the miracles of demons, which are performed by magic arts".[33] It is worth emphasizing here that the "non-true miracles" Aquinas is talking about can be described equally well as natural, demonic and magical – he attributes them to occult "forces of natural things" but then gives as an example "the miracles of demons, which are performed by magic arts". This idea that the demonic and the magical should be categorized as natural rather than supernatural or preternatural was to have a long future, forming the cornerstone of conventional demonological thinking in the era of the great witch-hunt. The fullest recent account of early modern demonology in English is insistent that demonology was considered by contemporaries "a form of natural knowledge" and that it is a fundamental mistake to associate the witchcraft beliefs of the time with "supernaturalism".[34]

---

[33] miracula facere, solius Dei est.... Cum igitur ab aliqua creatura miracula fieri videntur, vel non sunt vera miracula, quia fiunt per aliquas virtutes naturalium rerum, licet nobis occultas, sicut est de miraculis daemonum, quae magicis artibus fiunt; vel si sunt vera miracula, impetrantur per aliquem a Deo, ut scilicet talia operetur: *Compendium theologiae*, lib. 1, chapter 136 co., *Opera omnia* (as in note 9), 3, p. 615; cf. *Summa contra gentiles* 3. 102–7, ibid., 2, pp. 94–6.

[34] Stuart Clark, *Thinking with Demons: The Idea of Witchcraft in Early Modern Europe* (Oxford, 1997), pp. 168–9.

There were, however, alternative approaches to magic, which saw it, or at least some forms of it, as indeed natural but non-demonic. The heyday of the concept "natural magic" was to be in the sixteenth and seventeenth centuries, but it was not unknown in the medieval period, being employed notably by William of Auvergne, an impeccably orthodox figure – teacher of theology at Paris and bishop of Paris – whose main work, the modestly titled "On the Universe", dates, probably, from the 1230s.[35] William makes it clear that he regards "natural magic (*magica naturalis* or *magia naturalis*)" as quite innocent: "Those things worked by natural magic are not an offence against the Creator or a wrong, unless someone employs that art either too curiously or for evil."[36] Being "too curious" meant indulging in *curiositas*, that is, "the desire to know things that are not

---

[35] *Opera omnia* (2 vols., Orleans, 1674, reprint Frankfurt, 1963) 1, pp. 593–1074; some parts have been translated: William of Auvergne, *The Universe of Creatures*, tr. Roland J. Teske (Milwaukee, 1998). On William and magic, see Steven B. Marrone, "William of Auvergne on Magic in Natural Philosophy and Theology", in *Was ist Philosophie im Mittelalter?*, ed. Jan Aertsen and Andreas Speer (*Miscellanea Medievalia* 26, Berlin, 1998), pp. 741–8; Lynn Thorndike, *A History of Magic and Experimental Science during the First Thirteen Centuries of Our Era* (2 vols., New York, 1923) 2, chapter 52, pp. 338–71: "William of Auvergne". For his general views of Nature, Albrecht Quentin, *Naturkenntnisse und Naturanschauungen bei Wilhelm von Auvergne* (Hildesheim, 1976); there is a general summary in Roland J. Teske, "William of Auvergne", in *A Companion to Philosophy in the Middle Ages*, ed. Jorge J. E. Gracia and Timothy B. Noone (Malden, MA, and Oxford, 2003), pp. 680–7.

[36] De his autem, quae fiunt per magicam naturalem, scito quod nullam habent creatoris offensam, vel injuriam, nisi quis ex ea arte, vel nimis curiose, vel malum operetur: *De universo* (as in previous note) 1. 1. 46 (a – two successive chapters are numbered 46 in this edition), p. 663; the phrase *magia naturalis* occurs in his *De legibus* 24, in his *Opera omnia* (as in previous note) 1, pp. 18–102, at p. 69.

necessary" and might lead to such "unspeakable operations" as divination and fortune-telling.[37]

Properly directed, however, natural magic was, according to William, simply a branch of natural science. Its special sphere of activity is the wonderful works of nature, which in some ways its practitioners could develop. For instance, nature can generate frogs, lice, and worms suddenly, but assistance can be applied to strengthen and sharpen the process. Those ignorant of these methods presume that demonic aid must be being invoked, but

> those who are learned in these things are not amazed at such things but glorify the creator alone in them, knowing that nature works through his omnipotent will alone, both according to the custom known to men and beyond that custom, not only working in new ways but also producing new things.[38]

William's list of wonderful natural forces has some of the miscellaneous quality of Gervase of Tilbury's marvels: sealskin repels lightning; olive trees planted by virgins thrive much better; some people have a morbid fear of cats – "they are terrified at the sight of a cat", he says – *horrent aspectum catti* (and curiously such a phobia is recorded of one thirteenth-century monarch, Wenceslas II of Bohemia).[39] William of Auvergne has to tread a careful

---

[37] curiositate quae est libido sciendi non necessaria ... infandissima illa opera ... videlicet inspectio speculi, etc.: ibid. 24, p. 70.

[38] Qui autem in his docti sunt, talia non mirantur, sed solum creatorem in eis glorificant scientes, quod sola omnipotentissima voluntate ipsius natura operatur, et juxta consuetudinem notam hominibus et praeter consuetudinem non solum novis modis, sed etiam res novas: ibid. 24, p. 70.

[39] *De universo* (as in note 35) 1. 1. 46 (a – two successive chapters are numbered 46 in this edition), pp. 657–8; cf. the comment of a contemporary chronicler on Wencelas: catos videre eorumque garritum audire ex quadam consuetudine exhorruit: Peter of Zittau, *Chronicon Aule Regie* 1. 15, *Fontes Rerum Bohemicarum* 4, ed. J. Emler (Prague, 1884), pp. 1–337, at p. 22.

line: amulets are vain nonsense, but paschal wax images blessed by the pope ward off thunder; incantations are wicked but exorcisms work.[40]

The canonization processes of the later medieval period, already mentioned, were particularly focussed on sifting out anything that might be identified as natural or magical from supposed miracles. For, if, say, an apparent healing miracle could be explained by natural processes, perhaps medical, or had involved such illicit magical procedures as incantations, then it could be ruled out as a true miracle supporting the case for canonization. And demarcating the licit and illicit in such cases might be complex. How, for example, did one draw the line between legitimate invocation and prohibited incantation? Hostiensis, one of the great canon lawyers of the thirteenth century, insisted that it was a condition of a true miracle that it *not* be a result solely of the pronouncement of certain words – "not from the power of words (*non ex vi verborum*)".[41] He would perhaps have endorsed the distinction that anthropologists of earlier generations used to employ, between magic (coercive) and religion (propitiatory or supplicatory). Here the Victorian and Edwardian anthropologists and the thirteenth-century Scholastics had common ground.

It was thus not always a simple matter to spell out the difference, which we have seen Thomas Aquinas confronting, between true miracles and the marvellous feats of magicians and demons. A biblical example that proved a favourite peg on which to hang discussion of this topic was the contest between Moses and Aaron and the magicians of Egypt before Pharaoh described in the Book

---

[40] Thorndike, *History of Magic* (as in note 35), 2, pp. 352–3, drawing particularly on *De legibus* 27, pp. 84–9.

[41] Hostiensis (Henry de Segusio), *Summa aurea* (Lyons, 1548), III, sub rubrica "De reliquiis et veneratione sanctorum", fol. 188v.

2. MIRACLE OF RODS CHANGED INTO SERPENTS. The contest between Moses and Aaron on one hand and Pharaoh's magicians on the other, as described in Exodus 7, involved Aaron casting down his rod, which then became a serpent, and the magicians then casting down their rods, which also became serpents. Although Aaron's serpent swallowed up the other serpents, the passage still seemed to indicate that magicians could effect genuine transformations. The biblical passage thus proved a major stimulus to medieval discussion of the distinction between miracle and magic. (The Pierpont Morgan Library, New York. MS M.394, fol. 43v (Bible Historiale of Guyart des Moulins, ca. 1251-ca. 1297).)

of Exodus, chapter 7.[42] When Aaron threw down his rod, it became a serpent, but when the magicians threw down theirs, they became serpents too. Was there any difference?

We can see one of the leading scholars of the thirteenth century, Aquinas' teacher Albertus Magnus, almost becoming entangled with these serpents.[43] In his discussion of the question whether the conjurations of magicians are miracles, he first affirms that the activities of Pharaoh's magicians were true and not illusory; they really did change staffs into serpents. In a strict sense, however, these transformations were not miracles, he says, for it is natural for wood to turn into serpents (we leave aside the empirical issue here, because for Albertus it was an axiom that rotting trees generated serpents and dragons). All that happened in the case of Pharaoh's magicians was that this natural process was speeded up by the help of demons, who were able to do so through the subtlety and agility of their nature. This view left Albertus a little exposed, however. One of the most well-known biblical miracles was Christ turning water into wine, and was it not the case that water turned naturally into wine, through rainfall, absorption by the vine and so forth? It was a process at least as natural as wood turning into snakes. "But", argues Albertus, "Christ did not make wine from water in this way, but solely by the command of his will."[44] He then goes on to point out that it is not instantaneous action that constitutes a miracle,

---

[42] Caroline Bynum points out the that "the fullest scholastic treatments of the miraculous" address precisely such paradigmatic "species transformations" rather than cures, which are however "by far the most common miracle in actual miracle collections": Caroline Walker Bynum, *Metamorphosis and Identity* (New York, 2001), p. 90.

[43] Albertus Magnus, *Summa Theologica* 2. 8. 30. 1. 1, ed. A. Borgnet, *Opera omnia* 32 (Paris, 1895), pp. 319–23.

[44] Sed hoc modo Christus non fecit vinum ex aqua, sed solo imperio suae voluntatis... : ibid., p. 323.

but rather an event "raised above the order of nature". In any case, the magic transformations of Pharaoh's magicians were not instantaneous, he says, but, properly speaking, simply quicker than nature could produce and hence "wonders" not "miracles". The proliferation of argument here may remind one of the old adage, "Never believe anyone who gives you more than one reason why they can't do something." Albertus is evidently in some intellectual discomfort, havering as he considers the proper definition of miracle, in particular whether instantaneous effect or acceleration of natural processes are to be considered essential or irrelevant considerations.

When thinkers and writers of the medieval period deployed the language of "nature", they thus did so to make a range of possible points. Addressing the marvels of the natural world, they might declare how such things were indeed contrary to the usual course of nature but not to nature intrinsically, and hence they could still be clearly distinguished from divine miracles. Such natural oddities might amaze people (which was, of course, the heart of the Augustinian concept of miracle), but their causes were natural, even if unknown. They also had to steer a careful course in their thinking between the miraculous and the magical.

In general, one of the striking things in these discussions of the boundaries of the natural is how difficult it was for medieval thinkers to be consistently systematic on the subject. Concepts of nature and its opposites and exceptions, whether the latter be construed as miracle, marvel, monster or magic, are not susceptible to quick and easy definition, indeed not only for the thinkers of the medieval period but also for us. The categories and definitions used for discussing or referring to the natural and the supernatural were fluid, potentially contradictory, and often indeed unexamined.

Moreover, the vocabulary and terms of discussion of the natural and the supernatural did not develop in isolation but under the pressure of dogmatic constraints. One did not want a God who was unnatural. "Nature" had such a large and ancient associated baggage as a positive and normative concept that it was hard to classify anything God did as "contrary to nature". "The things that God does beyond the order of nature", Aquinas asserts, "are not contrary to nature."[45] God could indeed even be identified as "first nature (*prima natura*)" and hence his deeds were pre-eminently "natural".[46] Further, if to God all things were natural, then, of course, in a sense, there are no miracles. In the pithy statement of a thirteenth-century monk: "*we* call a miracle anything against the accustomed course of nature, which produces wonder in us; *according to the causes above*, nothing is a miracle."[47]

Let me now turn briefly to my final theme or, rather, question: was there a contraction of the sphere of the supernatural in the period, say, 1000–1500? A persuasive case can be made, although with such a vast topic, I focus only on a couple of selected component parts of that argument.

To take an example at random, let us turn to trial by ordeal. Ordeal, which was widespread in Latin Europe during the early and central Middle Ages, involved the resolution of a dispute

[45] Quod ea quae Deus facit praeter naturae ordinem non sunt contra naturam: Thomas Aquinas, *Summa contra Gentiles*, 3. 100, title, *Opera omnia* (as in note 9), 2, p. 94.

[46] Miracula . . . ab alio principio fiunt quam sit natura, scilicet a superiori et prima natura: Alexander of Hales, *Summa theologica* 2. 2. 3. 2. q. 3, tit. 3. 1, "de miraculis" (4 vols. in 5, plus index vol., Quarracchi, 1924–79) 2, p. 286. For the common phrase, "Natura, id est Deus", see Jacques Chiffoleau, "*Contra Naturam*: pour une approche casuistique et procédurale de la nature médiévale", *Micrologus* 4 (1996), pp. 265–312, at p. 285.

[47] Miraculum dicimus quicquid fit contra solitum cursum naturae, unde miramur. Secundum causas superiores miraculum nihil est: Caesarius of Heisterbach, *Dialogus miraculorum* 10. 1, ed. J. Strange (2 vols. and index, Cologne, etc., 1851–7) 2, p. 217.

not by the usual legal means of oath-swearing, the testimony of witnesses and the hearing of relevant evidence, but by submitting the accused or one of the parties in a civil suit to a dramatic physical test: carrying a red-hot iron, plucking a pebble from a boiling cauldron, being cast into a pool or stream. The result would determine the verdict. In the ordeals of hot iron and hot water, the hand had to be healing cleanly after a given period, usually three days; in the ordeal of cold water, the accused were deemed guilty if they floated, innocent if they sank (students especially like this apparent piece of imbecility, with its echoes of the mob in *Monty Python and the Holy Grail* calling out, "Throw her into the pond!", but, of course, the accused were fastened to a rope and pulled out if they sank). The underlying concept of trial by ordeal was not a random test but a carefully staged ritual in which God would give his verdict, and *iudicium Dei*, "judgment of God", was in fact a standard medieval term for ordeal.

Trial by ordeal virtually disappeared from Latin Europe by 1300, and several great scholars have been willing to see its passing as part of a "process of limiting the scope of the appeal to the supernatural in human affairs" and a sign of a new "disengagement of the sacred from the profane", involving a "sharpening and delimitation of the role of the supernatural".[48] Some of the debate that took place about trial by ordeal in the twelfth and thirteenth centuries was indeed couched in terms of the natural and the supernatural. Those who thought that trial by ordeal seemed to require the elements to behave in an unusual way, hot

[48] Richard W. Southern, *The Making of the Middle Ages* (London and New Haven, 1953), p. 98; Peter Brown, "Society and the Supernatural: A Medieval Change", *Daedalus* 104 (1975), pp. 133–51, at pp. 135, 147 (repr. in his *Society and the Holy in Late Antiquity* (Berkeley and Los Angeles, 1982), pp. 302–32).

iron not burning the innocent, water not submerging the guilty, might question whether God wished to "compel the nature of things to yield to" merely human requirements.[49] Other opponents mocked these "ordeal miracles"[50] and stressed that they were given credence only by simple people ignorant of the natural order.[51] Others thought that it was wrong to demand supernatural results. Ordeal was illicit according to Aquinas because "a miraculous effect is expected of God".[52] In all this polemic, the anomalous place of ordeal in the landscape of the natural and the miraculous was an important point.

Another big area where one might look, when considering changes in the conceptualization of the natural and the supernatural, is the enormous transformation in the educational curriculum that took place in western Europe between 1150 and 1250.

Latin Europe was, for most of the Middle Ages, ignorant of Greek.[53] Scholars in western Europe thus had no access to the works of Plato, Aristotle and the other ancient Greek philosophers unless they had been translated into Latin, and, for a long time, few of them were, the main exceptions being some of

---

[49] ut quibuslibet eorum votis rerum naturam cedere compellat: Saxo Grammaticus, *Gesta Danorum* 14. 54. 20, ed. J. Olrik and H. Raeder (2 vols., Copenhagen, 1931–57), p. 508.

[50] miracula peregrini judicii: Peter the Chanter, *Verbum abbreviatum* 78, *Patrologia latina* 205, cols. 23–270, at col. 228.

[51] Leges, que a quibusdam simplicibus sunt dicte paribiles, qui nec rerum naturam respiciunt nec veritatem attendunt: Frederick II, *Constitutions of Melfi* 2. 31, ed. Wolfgang Stürner, *Die Konstitutionen Friedrichs II. für das Königreich Sizilien, Monumenta Germaniae Historica, Constitutiones et acta publica imperatorum et regum* 2, suppl. (Hanover, 1996), p. 337.

[52] expectatur aliquis miraculosus effectus a Deo: Thomas Aquinas, *Summa Theologiae* 2. 2. 95. 8 ad 3, *Opera omnia* (as in note 9), 2, p. 650.

[53] See Walther Berschin, *Greek Letters and the Latin Middle Ages* (Eng. tr., Washington, DC, 1988).

Aristotle's elementary works on logic. From around 1100, this changed dramatically as ever increasing numbers of works of Greek science and philosophy were translated, notably but by no means only Aristotle's works. The tale of what happened when these works did arrive in Paris, Europe's leading academic centre, is remarkable, involving as it does one of the most dramatic reversals in European intellectual history. Aristotle's logical works were uncontroversial, but his works on biology, psychology, physics, and so on, which bore the significant collective title *libri naturales*, "the books about natural things", were initially viewed with suspicion by the ecclesiastical authorities. In 1210, they were even banned in the nascent university of Paris: "the books of Aristotle on natural philosophy and the commentaries on them shall not be read at Paris, in public or in private, and this under pain of excommunication".[54] It is therefore rather poignant to read an account of the basic arts syllabus at Paris from 1255: after the introductory lectures on logic and grammar had been given, the teachers were to turn to lecturing on "Aristotle's Physics, Metaphysics and the book On Animals . . . the book On the Heavens, books one and four of the Meteorology . . . the book On the Soul . . . the book Sense and Sensibilia . . . the book On Sleep . . . ", and so on.[55] Aristotle's books on nature had gone from proscribed texts to prescribed texts in a generation or so.

---

[54] nec libri Aristotelis de naturali philosophia nec commenta legantur Parisius publice vel secreto, et hoc sub pena excommunicationis inhibemus: *Chartularium Universitatis Parisiensis* 1 (*1200–1286*), ed. Henri Denifle (Paris, 1889), no. 11, p. 70.

[55] Physicam Aristotelis, metaphysicam et librum de animalibus . . . librum celi et mundi, librum primum metheorum cum quarto . . . librum de anima . . . librum de sensu et sensato . . . librum de sompno et vigilia . . . : ibid., no. 246, p. 278.

What the works of Aristotle, along with the other Greek and Arabic texts which were translated in this period, offered the Latin West was something new – systematic, naturalistic, and rationalistic analysis of the world from a non-Christian viewpoint. There was a certain audaciousness in making this the foundation course in the universities of Catholic Europe.

It would be possible to argue that the adoption of Aristotelianism in the great centres of higher study in medieval Europe should be interpreted as a big step towards a more naturalistic world view. One could seek to illustrate this from most branches of study (for Aristotle is famously impressive on subjects as diverse as metaphysics and the ink sac of the cuttlefish), but perhaps the strongest apparent case emerges from his *Politics*. Aristotle's *Politics* was translated into Latin by the Dominican William of Moerbeke around 1260 and quickly became the subject of commentaries by Albertus Magnus, Aquinas, and others. Probably the most familiar phrase from the *Politics* is Aristotle's dogmatic statement that "man is by nature a political animal (*politikon zoon*)".[56] In William of Moerbeke's translation "*politikon zoon*" becomes "*civile animal*", an animal naturally civic, and Aquinas elaborates, "it is natural for man to be a social and political animal".[57] All this makes it plausible to argue, as a distinguished historian of medieval thought has done, that "The

---

[56] I would normally use the translation "human being" rather than "man" but Aristotle has just been at pains to point out how we should be sure to distinguish women from slaves, so perhaps the more gender-specific term is appropriate here.

[57] Aristotle, *Politics* 1253a 2; homo natura civile animal est: William of Moerbeke's translation, in Aristotle, *Politicorum libri octo cum vetusta translatione Guilelmi de Moerbeka*, ed. F. Susemihl (Leipzig, 1872), p. 7. Naturale autem est homini ut sit animal sociale et politicum: Thomas Aquinas, *De regno* (*De regimine principum*) 1. 1, *Opera omnia* (as in note 9) 3, p. 595.

recovery of Aristotle's natural philosophy led people to take note of the naturalness of the political community itself".[58] The birth or rebirth of political thought premised on the naturalness of the human political community can be set alongside the disappearance of ordeal, the judgment of God, in legal process as another instance of that limitation of the supernatural that has been mentioned.

The great German sociologist of the early twentieth century Max Weber used the phrase "disenchantment of the world" to describe what he saw as the special path the West had taken, marked by the growing dominance of rationalism and an increasingly instrumental attitude to the natural world. It is a viewpoint that harmonizes easily with some modern environmentalist critiques of western civilization. Amongst professional historians, at least among those prepared to make rash generalizations, Weber's phrase is usually applied specifically to the period from the sixteenth to the eighteenth centuries, with the rise of modern science and the Enlightenment as uncontentious contributors to the disenchantment, and Protestantism and capitalism as less certain members of the cast. However, it is clear that Weber himself believed this process had been going on in the West not for centuries but for millennia.[59] Hence, if we take this seriously, the medieval period could be viewed not as the cartoon "Other" to modern pragmatic rationalist society but as a stage on the path to it. The German original of Weber's "disenchantment of the world" is "die Entzauberung der Welt". *Zauber* is the usual

---

[58] David Luscombe, "The State of Nature and the Origin of the State", in *The Cambridge History of Later Medieval Philosophy*, ed. Norman Kretzmann, Anthony Kenny, and Jan Pinborg (Cambridge, 1982), pp. 757–70, at p. 761.

[59] dieser in der okzidentalen Kultur durch Jahrtausende fortgesetzte Entzauberungsprozess . . . : *Wissenschaft als Beruf* (Stuttgart, 1995), p. 19 (originally published Munich and Leipzig, 1919).

German word for magic, so the literal sense of the phrase is "taking the magic out of the world". Perhaps those who opposed and eventually prohibited trial by ordeal or those who introduced the new natural sciences to European universities can be seen as agents busily taking the magic out of the world.

Historical issues of this degree of generality can, of course, never be resolved conclusively, no matter how much evidence is piled up. However, if we wanted suddenly to turn devil's advocate – an appropriate metaphor in fact – and argue an opposite case, one of our prime exhibits would be the great witch persecutions, which were not, or were barely, medieval, but, rather, characteristic of the early modern period.

It is indeed one of the most perplexing aspects of early modern European history that the centuries to which historians have given such labels as the Renaissance and the Age of Discovery, the same period which saw the rise of modern science, coincided with the age of the mass witch-hunt. Historians generally like their period labels clear-cut. How many books, for instance, are titled "Age of . . . " something – Absolutism, Adversity, Affluence, Anxiety (especially popular), and that is only the beginning of the "A"s. These "Ages" are difficult to match with complex realities, however. How does one reconcile the picture of a new dawn in European history, marked by such glories as the art of Leonardo, the scientific breakthroughs of Copernicus and Galileo, and the literary genius of Shakespeare with the hard fact that at this very period, tens of thousands of women and men were executed by the courts for copulating with demons, eating babies, and flying to midnight orgies?

"The Machine of This World"

Ideas of the Physical Universe

G IVING THIS SECOND CHAPTER THE TITLE I HAVE IN-
volves some sleight of hand. I intend to organize it
around the issue admirably summed up in the title of an important book in the history of science, namely, *The Mechanization of
the World Picture*. It is obviously one of those attractive books for
which the thesis is so clear from the title that you may not feel it
necessary to read it. The author was Eduard Jan Dijksterhuis, and
the book was originally published in Dutch in 1950 and appeared
in English translation in 1961.[1] Dijksterhuis argued that of all the
changes that have occurred in "scientific thought about nature",
one of the most important was "the emergence of the conception of the world usually called mechanical or mechanistic".[2]
Although he gives some serious consideration to the ancient
Greeks and finds the Scholastic physicists of the fourteenth century interesting, the core of his story concerns what happened in
the sixteenth and seventeenth centuries, culminating in Newton:
"With the appearance of Newton's *Principia* . . . the mechanization of the world-picture had in principle been accomplished."
Definition of "mechanization" is not, however, a simple matter.

---

[1] *De mechanisering van het Wereldbeeld* (Amsterdam, 1950); *The Mechanization of the World Picture* (Oxford, 1961).

[2] Ibid., p. 3.

Dijksterhuis explicitly says that it is misleading to stress merely "the conception according to which the physical universe is seen as a great machine".[3] Newton's concept of force, for instance, which is a central feature of his system, was rejected by several of his contemporaries, on reasonable grounds, as "essentially unmechanistic".[4] What was vital, according to Dijksterhuis, was "the introduction of a description of nature with the aid of the mathematical concepts of classical mechanics".[5]

When asking, as I will, if there were any elements in medieval thinking about the universe that made sense for it to be termed "a machine", I clearly do not wish to imply that any medieval thinkers conceived of the world in the terms of Newtonian physics. Yet if we take the most common caricature of the New-tonian system – and one still frequently used pedagogically – that is, a universe of billiard balls, and ask, was there a strand in medieval thinking that corresponded to this cartoon picture, then a case can be made.

The original meaning of the word machine given in the *Oxford English Dictionary* is "a fabric or structure, especially the fabric of the universe", and the same source defines fabric as "a product of skilled workmanship". In this sense, there certainly were many medieval thinkers and writers who saw the physical universe as a machine. In fact the phrase in my chapter title, "the machine of this world (*machina mundi*)" was widespread among Christian Latin writers from an early period, although it had classical roots and was not distinctively Christian.[6] The Anglo-Saxon poet Aldhelm writes, "God Almighty . . . from whom proceeded the whole machine of the present world".[7] Yet what he

---

[3] Ibid., p. 495.   [4] Ibid., p. 497.

[5] Ibid., p. 501.

[6] It had been used by Lucretius (5. 96), for example.

[7] Deus omnipotens . . . a quo processit praesentis machina mundi: *De virgini-tate (Carmen)*, lines 1678–9, ed. Rudolf Ehwald, *Monumenta Germaniae*

meant by this might simply be "the structure that God has created", with no implication of mechanical movement. So the sleight of hand I confess to is in translating the common medieval Latin phrase *machina mundi* as "the machine of this world", for perhaps a false impression might be conveyed.

On the other hand, there are two elements which might bring the medieval notion of "the machine of this world" a little nearer to the billiard-ball universe of the Newtonian caricature. For what that billiard-ball picture is intended to convey is a universe that can be explained in terms of matter in motion, and in the medieval period there were influential theories that stressed the explanatory importance of just those things: matter and motion. Indeed one medieval definition of the subject matter of "natural science" was "the mobile body".[8] So it is worth asking how far such explanations could go in the medieval period and, of

---

Historica, Auctores antiquissimi 15 (Berlin, 1919), pp. 350–471, at p. 423. The word *machina* is a favourite of Aldhelm's, occurring 24 times in his works.

[8] In scientia naturali est consideratio de corpore mobili sicut de subiecto: cited from BL Royal 12 G. II (s. xiii ex.), fol. 1v (as fol.2), by Charles Burnett, "The Introduction of Aristotle's Natural Philosophy into Great Britain: A Preliminary Survey of the Manuscript Evidence", in John Marenbon (ed.), *Aristotle in Britain during the Middle Ages* (Turnhout, 1996), pp. 21–50, at p. 46, with reference to similar passages. Compare Aquinas' commentary on Aristotle's *De celo*: scientia naturalis est de rebus naturalibus: ergo scientia naturalis consistit circa corpora et magnitudines... Naturalis quidem considerat de corporibus inquantum sunt mobilia: Thomas Aquinas, *In De caelo*, 1. 1. 1–2, *Opera omnia*, ed. Roberto Busa (7 vols., Stuttgart-Bad Cannstatt, 1980) 4, p. 1. The beginning of the commentary on Aristotle's *On Generation and Corruption* by Geoffrey of Aspall (d. 1287) reads "the subject of natural philosophy is mobile bodies considered in general" (as cited in translation from Oxford, Merton College MS 272, fol. 176, by John E. Murdoch and Edith D. Sylla, in David C. Lindberg (ed.), *Science in the Middle Ages* (Chicago, 1978), p. 206, with the author's name as "Geoffrey of Haspyl").

course, what problems and alternative models limited the idea of a universe of matter and motion.

According to Peter Lombard, whose theological text-book the *Sentences* was mentioned in the first chapter, during the first three days of Creation "the machine of all this world was arranged and its parts organized".[9] He goes on to specify: "In those days (i.e., the first three) the four elements of the world were differentiated and arranged in their places. In the following three days those four elements were adorned."[10] This is the first strongly physical component of the machine of the universe – it is made of up four material elements. These were earth, air, fire, and water, and a great deal about the world could be explained by their characteristic features, their location, and admixtures. The elements were the general and standard foundation of all medieval physical thought, and these physical components, the elements, were in motion. Isidore of Seville, the great ency-clopaedist of the early Middle Ages, put the issue succinctly: "The universe consists of the heavens and the earth, the sea and all the stars. It is called the universe (*mundus*) because it is always in motion (*motu*) for no rest is given to its elements."[11] Setting aside the highly speculative – not to say improbable – etymology here, Isidore quite simply presents the universe as elements in motion.

[9] disposita est universitatis huius mundi machina, et partibus suis distributa: *Sententiae in IV libris distinctae* 2. 14. 9, ed. Collegium S. Bonaventurae (3rd ed., 2 vols., Spicilegium Bonaventurianum 4–5, Grottaferrata, 1971–81) 1, p. 399.

[10] Quatuor ergo mundi elementa illis diebus, suis locis distincta sunt et ordi-nata. Tribus autem sequentibus diebus ornata sunt illa quatuor elementa: ibid.

[11] Mundus est is qui constat ex caelo, [et] terra et mare cunctisque sideribus. Qui ideo mundus est appellatus, quia semper in motu est; nulla enim requies eius elementis concessa est: *Etymologiae* 3. 29, ed. W. M. Lindsay (2 vols., Oxford, 1911), unpaginated.

If Isidore provided the standard encyclopaedia for the early Middle Ages, then it was John of Sacrobosco, or John of Holywood, writing around 1230, who gave generations of students, from the thirteenth to the seventeenth century, their introduction to astronomy. His *Treatise on the Sphere* enjoyed a truly Hollywood celebrity. "No scientific work from the middle ages has ever enjoyed a similar popularity", reads his entry in the new *Dictionary of National Biography*.[12] He uses the standard phrase "*universalis mundi machina*", which his translator, Lynn Thorndike, rendered as "the machine of the universe",[13] but I mention him only to point to the title of his work – *Treatise on the Sphere*. It was basic medieval cosmology to posit a universe of moving spheres, even if the billiard-ball analogy was not, to my knowledge, ever employed. Here, along with elementary theory, is another idea of the physical universe as matter in motion.

Medieval thinkers interested in physical explanation of nature could thus employ both the logic of the elements and the logic of the spheres. In this chapter, I give an example of each, first one dealing mainly with the issue of the physical elements, then one concerned with the movements of the spheres, in each case stressing, as already mentioned, problems and alternative models.

My first case study concerns the distribution of the elements, specifically earth and water, in this physical globe we inhabit, "the earth" as we call it. I look at three moments, one each from the eleventh, twelfth, and fourteenth centuries, and my story begins in the garden of a great church in Alsace one day in the 1080s. Here Manegold of Lautenbach, a German scholar

---

[12] Olaf Pedersen, "Sacrobosco, John de (d. c.1236)", *Oxford Dictionary of National Biography* (Oxford, 2004) 48, pp. 549–50.
[13] John de Sacrobosco, *Tractatus de spera* 1, ed. Lynn Thorndike, 'The Sphere' of Sacrobosco and Its Commentators (Chicago, 1949), p. 78.

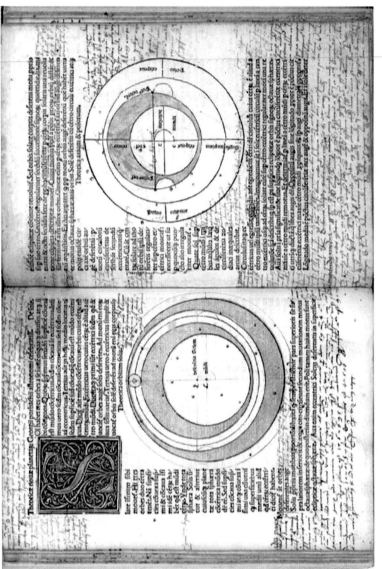

3. SPHERES. The *Treatise on the Sphere* by John of Sacrobosco, or John of Holywood, writing around 1230, provided the principal introduction to astronomy for students for hundreds of years. It is a short, clear description of the medieval cosmological system, in which the earth formed the central sphere in a concentric universe. The workings of the universe are explained by the motion of physical bodies. (University of Toronto, Stillman Drake collection, annotated printed edition of Sacrobosco's *Sphere*.)

and ecclesiastic, was strolling with an acquaintance, Wolfhelm of Cologne, talking about books, "as scholars do".[14] The subject of Macrobius, the late Roman author, came up and produced violent disagreement. "You", writes Manegold in the polemic he later directed against Wolfhelm, "argued that the philosophers and Macrobius . . . had said few things with which you disagreed, I, on the other hand, asserted that I had found many things in them that were contrary to our faith and salvation."[15]

A specific instance of the ancient natural philosophy that Manegold so distrusted concerns the geography, especially the human geography, of the globe. Macrobius, the ancient author who had been the catalyst of such a stormy discussion in the gardens of Lautenbach, had transmitted knowledge of many geographical and cosmological theories of the ancient world to his medieval readers. Amongst these was the idea that there are four habitable areas of dry land in the world, two in the Northern Hemisphere and two in the Southern, which are completely cut off from each other by impassable ocean and by the uninhabitable torrid zone around the equator.[16] Postulating several unknown and unknowable *habitable* regions might seem fairly neutral; postulating unknowable *inhabited* regions was not and already in late antiquity such a theory had been identified as contrary to Bible history and the Christian faith. Scripture posited

---

[14] more scolarium: Manegold of Lautenbach, *Liber contra Wolfelmum*, pref., ed. Wilfried Hartmann, *Monumenta Germaniae Historica, Quellen zur Geistesgeschichte des Mittelalters* 8 (Weimar, 1972), p. 39. For dating, and discussion of whether the setting is simply a *topos*, see Hartmann's introduction, pp. 12–15.

[15] tu pauca, que tibi displicerent, philosophos et Macrobium . . . dixisse contenderes, ego econtra plurima fidei et saluti nostre contraria in ipsis me invenisse assererem: ibid., pp. 39–40.

[16] Macrobius, *In Somnium Scipionis* 2. 5, ed. Mireille Armisen-Marchetti (2 vols., Paris, 2003) 2, pp. 22–30, with full annotation.

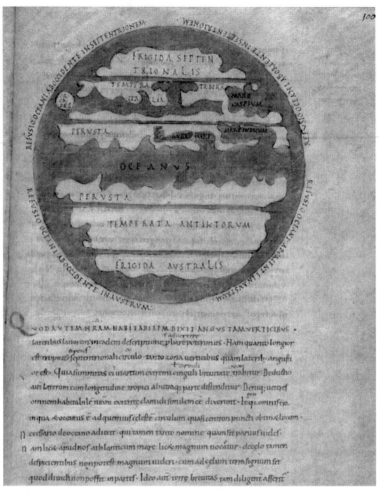

4. MACROBIUS WORLD MAP. Macrobius, a late Roman author who wrote a Commentary on Cicero's *Dream of Scipio*, transmitted various ancient geographical theories to the Middle Ages. Amongst the most controversial was the idea that there could be human beings living in the antipodes, although cut off from our own northern habitable zone by an impassably hot equatorial barrier. This map, illustrating Macrobius' Commentary, shows the frigid polar zones, the impassably hot zones, and the northern and southern temperate zones; the former labels the Orkneys and Italy, the latter is titled "Temperata Antiktorum", that is, "the temperate region of the inhabitants of the opposite side of the earth". (Bodleian Library, University of Oxford, MS. D'Orville 77, fol. 100; German, tenth or eleventh century.)

the unitary descent of all human beings and a unitary salvation history. Neither was compatible with four races of humans who were completely cut off from each other. St Augustine had made this point clearly.[17]

This is the issue that Manegold takes up in his attack on Wolfhelm, and it is worth citing his words at length, for they reveal not only the grounds for his objection to the four-region theory but also the rhetorical weaponry he wielded with such vigour. He writes

> For once you accept that there are four regions inhabited by human beings, between which there can be absolutely no prospect of natural contact, say, do, how it will be true, what the holy and apostolic Church rightly confesses, namely that the saviour, who was foretold by our first fathers from, so to speak, the infancy of this world, and subsequently prefigured in multiple and many plain ways by the patriarchs and prophets, came at length in the fullness of time, made known and revealed by his wonderful works of humility and love, for the salvation of the whole human race, if three races of human beings are excluded, which this Macrobius argues there can be, besides this habitable region in which we live because of the temperateness of the zones of heaven and earth, and to whom knowledge of salvation could not come.[18]

---

[17] *De civitate dei* 16. 9, ed. B. Dombart and A. Kalb (2 vols., Corpus Christianorum, series latina 47–8, 1955), vol. 48, pp. 510–11.

[18] Suscepto enim semel, quattuor habitationes hominum esse, quorum ad se invicem nulla penitus possit esse per naturam commeandi licentia, dic, age, quomodo verum erit, quod sancta et apostolica racionabiliter confitetur ecclesia, salvatorem videlicet, per primos patres ab ipsis, ut ita dicam, huius mundi cunabulis presignatum et a patriarchis et prophetis consequenter multipharie et multis evidentibus modis prefiguratum, tandem in plenitudinem temporis ineffabilibus humilitatis et caritatis sue operibus cognitum et clarificatum in salutem tocius humani generis advenisse, si tria hominum genera excepta sunt, que predictus Macrobius preter hanc

Manegold's sentence is long, but his point is clear: Christ came to save all, and the Christian message has to be preached to the whole of humanity. How can this be done if there are groups of humans completely and permanently cut off from each other? Our picture of the human geography of the globe and the distribution of the continents has to fit in with biblical assumptions.

Manegold's diatribe against ancient philosophers – "the devil's seminary" as he called them[19] – is harnessed, perhaps strangely in our eyes, to a defence of Gregory VII, the great leader of the eleventh-century papacy, against his German enemies. Indeed, Manegold seems to have seen the struggle against the emperor Henry IV and other adversaries of pope Gregory, the so-called Investiture Conflict, and the fight against pagan philosophy as two parts of a wider battle. Chapter 22 of his treatise, pointing out the dangers of relying on non-Christian writers, is followed immediately by a chapter lamenting the fact that the Germans had withdrawn their obedience from the Roman Church.[20] It would be beyond the scope of this chapter, but it would be an interesting inquiry to see how views about the physical universe and political stances correlated among scholars of the medieval period.

A hundred years after Manegold, another scholar, like Manegold an Augustinian canon, but writing not in a German monastery but in the Paris of early Scholasticism, was pondering exactly the same issue as had disturbed the quiet of the gardens of Lautenbach. In a passage in his *Microcosmus*,

habitabilem quam incolimus secundum zonarum celi et terre temperiem posse esse persuadet, ad que tante salubritatis noticia pervenire non potuit?: Manegold, *Liber* (as in note 14) 4, pp. 51–2.

[19] diaboli seminario: ibid. 9, p. 62.

[20] Ibid. 22–3, pp. 93–105.

Godfrey[21] of St Victor considered the verse in Genesis where God says, "Let the waters under the heaven be gathered together unto one place and let the dry land appear". Immediately Godfrey alerts us that there is a difference of opinion concerning this matter between the theologian and the philosopher: according to Genesis, he says, adding "and the fathers of the catholic faith agree on this", "dry land appeared in one place only in the world", the rest remaining covered in water; "on the other hand, however, the natural philosopher asserts, with very credible reasoning, that four areas of dry land appeared in four places in the world and that each of them is not only habitable but inhabited."[22] Macrobius' position is clearly apparent here.

Despite the plausibility he concedes to the natural philosophers' arguments, however, Godfrey of St Victor thinks their views on this subject both wrong and dangerous. In order to demonstrate the falsehood of their position, he says he will use two kinds of approach: "First we will employ divine authority to convince those who maintain this opinion, then we will refute this assertion of theirs by another of their assertions."[23] The first part of the task is simple – Godfrey simply repeats the verse from Genesis. The second part involves him in a little basic physics.

---

[21] Sometimes called Geoffrey. For his life and writings, see Philippe Delhaye, *Le Microcosmus de Godefroy de Saint-Victor: étude théologique* (Lille and Gembloux, 1951), pp. 15–33. Delhaye dates the *Microcosmus* to c. 1185.

[22] Ex his enim dictis moysi, cui et catholice fidei patres assensum prebuerunt, videtur in uno tantummodo loco mundi aridam apparuisse, ceterasque terre partes universas continuatis aquis coopertas esse. E contra autem naturalis philosophus probabili valde ratione in quatuor locis mundi quatuor aridas asserit apparuisse et singulas non solum habitabiles sed et habitatas esse: Godefroy de Saint-Victor, *Microcosmus* 1. 46, ed. Philippe Delhaye (Lille and Gembloux, 1951), pp. 66–7.

[23] primum auctoritate divina huius opinionis assertores convincemus, deinde ex alia eorum assertione hanc ipsorum assertionem refellemus: ibid. 1. 48, p. 68.

As mentioned, it was a commonplace view in the ancient and medieval periods that there were four elements, earth, air, fire, and water. The heaviest was earth, then water, next air and fire. Elements sought their natural place, with the heaviest coming to rest in the lowest place, that is, the centre of the universe, the second heaviest finding its place around the heaviest, and so on. The natural disposition of the elements would thus be as follows: a spherical earth at the centre, completely surrounded by a sphere of water, which would be surrounded by a sphere of air and finally an outermost sphere of fire.

It was obvious to the senses that this model did not correspond to reality. Human life would be difficult if the earth were entirely encompassed in a sphere of water. Yet that seemed to be a necessary consequence of the basic assumptions about the physics of the elements. Attempts to explain this discrepancy between theory and observation were a perennial feature of intellectual life in any of the traditions that adopted the four-element theory, ancient, patristic, Muslim, and medieval.[24] However, Godfrey of St Victor was not interested in creating a consistent naturalistic theory about the distribution of earth and water in the universe. Quite the opposite. He raises this issue to refute any naturalistic explanation of the patterns of dry land.

The idea of four regions of dry land does not make sense, he says, given the nature of the elements – the earth should in theory be completely submerged. But then nor does the idea of one region of dry land. "How", asks Godfrey, "are the bonds of

---

[24] Giuseppe Boffito, "Intorno alla 'Quaestio de aqua et terra' attribuita a Dante I: La controversia dell'acqua e della terra prima e dopo di Dante", *Memorie della Reale Accademia delle Scienze di Torino*, 2nd ser., 51 (1902), pp. 73–159; Arnold Norlind, *Das Problem des gegenseitigen Verhältnisses von Land und Wasser und seine Behandlung im Mittelalter* (Lund, 1918); Delhaye, *Le Microcosmus... étude théologique* (as in note 21), pp. 282–6.

the proportions of the elements maintained, if earth, despising its middle position, should go beyond its bounds into the air".[25] The only way that dry land could exist on earth is through the direct command of God. "For what nature is it that earth, which is naturally heavier than water, should appear above the water, unless nature had surrendered at God's command?"[26] He revels in this transgression of physical laws, playing on the Latin verb *excedere*, "to go beyond the bounds": "Neither the things that go beyond their bounds nor those things whose bounds are transcended are of such kind that they can go beyond their bounds or be transcended naturally, unless the lord of nature had commanded that this transgression of the bounds should happen beyond the order of nature."[27]

In a sense Godfrey has a strong concept of nature. He certainly knows what it means for the elements to behave naturally and explicitly mentions "the order of nature". Yet in another sense, he is strongly "supernaturalist" and would doubtless have used the word "supernatural" if it had yet been invented. He distinguishes three kinds of action, divine, natural, and human, and, for him, the appearance of dry land is clearly one of the first type, "the works of God without the ministration of nature".[28] It may perhaps not be unfair to point out that Godfrey's starting point, the attempt to refute the claims of natural philosophers that there are four regions of dry land in the world, has rather

---

[25] Quomodo enim elementarium proportionum ligatura constaret, si terra, spreto medio vel mediis suis, usque ad aerem . . . excederet?: Godfrey, *Microcosmus* (as in note 22) 1. 51, p. 70.

[26] Que enim natura est ut terra naturaliter ponderosior aqua appareat super aquam, nisi imperanti deo cessisset natura?: ibid. 1. 49, pp. 68–9.

[27] Neque enim excedentia vel excessa sunt ut excedere se vel excedi a se naturaliter vel in parte possint, nisi nature dominus hanc excedentiam preter ordinem nature fieri inperasset: ibid. 1. 51, p. 70.

[28] opera dei sine ministerio nature: ibid. 1. 49, p. 68.

been lost sight of. Having established that the existence of *any* dry land is a result of direct divine action outside and beyond nature, there still remains the empirical question of how many pieces of dry land did God decide to uncover. Couldn't he have chosen to uncover four?

Although both Manegold, the Lautenbach polemicist, and Godfrey insist on scriptural authority for geographical assertions, their approaches differ. Manegold thunders his denunciations, but Godfrey also wants to play the natural philosophers at their own game, using the premises of contemporary physics to undermine the very possibility of a naturalistic explanation of the physical world we know. If the distribution of land and sea on the face of the globe can only be explained by direct divine intervention, then nature might indeed be said to have "surrendered".

My third and final example of a medieval writer grappling with this problem of the distribution of land and water on the globe comes from Italy in the early fourteenth century. Although his short treatise "On the location and shape of the two elements of water and earth" will be our main focus here, the author is actually better known for some of his other writings, such as the *Divine Comedy*. He is, of course, the poet Dante, who, in addition to his great poetic opus, explored various theories on the distribution of the elements in a short work written during his exile, in 1320.[29]

In his treatise, Dante cites few biblical texts and concentrates entirely on the physical arguments, as he himself emphasises: "the present treatise is limited to natural matter", he writes, using a phrase, "natural matter", which could refer equally well to "matter" in the sense of "the physical stuff of the universe"

---

[29] Dante Alighieri, *De situ et forma aque et terre*, ed. Giorgio Padoan (*Opere di Dante* 8/3, Florence 1968).

and in the sense of "subject matter". He then elaborates: the treatise is "limited to natural matter because it concerns only mobile being, namely water and earth, which are natural bodies."[30] He investigates various theories that would explain why water does not in fact completely surround the earth, as elemental theory would seem to require. Much of his energy goes into refuting the idea that the sphere of earth and the sphere of water might have different centres, so that their perimeters would overlap, leaving part of the sphere of earth protruding from the sphere of water. This was in fact quite an elegant solution to the problem, although it did involve the controversial idea that the centre of the universe was not also the centre of the spheres of each of the elements. Dante is unhappy with this idea. He postulates what would happen in such a cosmos when a lump of earth and a quantity of water were placed at the same point in space beyond the sphere of earth and water. Natural gravity would draw the lump of earth to the centre of the sphere of earth and the water to the centre of the sphere of water, but they would have to follow different trajectories because the two spheres did not share a common centre. "This", writes Dante, "not only is impossible, but Aristotle would laugh if he heard of it."[31]

Another argument Dante advances against the idea of two spheres with different centres was the actual configuration of the known world, that is, the land-mass of Europe, Africa, and Asia, which, in his view, consisted of dry land forming a rough semicircle. If the earth and the water formed two overlapping spheres, then the area of dry land would have to be circular, a piece of

[30] Tractatus presens est intra materiam naturalem, quia inter ens mobile, scilicet aquam et terram, que sunt corpora naturalia: ibid. 20, p. 30.

[31] quod non solum est impossibile, sed rideret Aristotiles si audiret: ibid. 12, p. 14. The phrase "rideret Aristotiles" is proverbial and used elsewhere by Dante: Convivio 4. 15. 6, ed. Franca Brambilla Ageno, Convivio: Testo (Opere di Dante 3/2, Florence, 1995), p. 358.

simple geometry that, Dante says, "should be self-evident, even to women",[32] the great Italian poet showing himself here a little more progressive than a recent president of Harvard. Dante's own position is that the spheres of earth and water do have a common centre but that there is a lump or hump in the sphere of the earth, bringing the habitable part of the world above the surface of the water, and the cause of this protuberance is the influence of the stars. His premises, methods, and conclusions are entirely naturalistic, even if he preserves the regularity of nature only by distinguishing a "simple nature", according to which all earth will seek the lowest spot, from a "universal nature", which actually shapes the physical universe as we know it, lumps and all.[33]

The apparent evolution from a purely theological viewpoint in Manegold, to a theological viewpoint which also seeks to deal with physical theories in Godfrey of St Victor, to a purely naturalistic discussion in Dante is striking, but we should perhaps remind ourselves that both Manegold and Godfrey were consciously attempting to refute contemporaries who espoused physicalist theories. This story may reflect a never-ending debate rather than the irresistible progress of western science.

I now turn from discussion of the configuration of the globe to the movements of the spheres. In a world without artificial

[32] sicut manifestum esse potest etiam mulieribus: Dante, *De situ* (as in note 29) 19, p. 28.

[33] licet terra secundum simplicem eius naturam equaliter petat centrum . . . secundum tamen naturam quondam patitur elevari in parte, Nature universali obediens: ibid. 19, p. 26. One should also note Dante's view in *Inferno* 34. 121–6, ed. Giorgio Petrocchi, *La commedia secondo l'antica vulgata* 2 (*Opere di Dante* 7/2, reprint, Florence, 1994), pp. 596–7: when Satan fell into the Southern Hemisphere, the land there withdrew to the Northern Hemisphere; simultaneously Mount Purgatory emerged from the earth that was shot out from the centre of the earth. The relationship between this passage and the *De situ* is one of the topics discussed in Klaus Ley, "Dante als Wissenschaftler: die 'Quaestio de aqua et terra'", *Deutsches Dantes Jahrbuch* 58 (1983), pp. 41–71.

light, average knowledge of the patterns of the heavens would obviously be far more profound and instinctive than in the modern world, even in those regions of northern Europe where the undimmed glory of the skies might occasionally be clouded over. Any brief examination, for example, of the annals and chronicles composed in the medieval period will show how deeply interested their composers and compilers were in astronomical phenomena. In fact, the early Irish annals have been singled out for their sustained series of observations, with the *Annals of Ulster* receiving the accolade as "the richest source of observations and the most accurate chronologically".[34] Amongst the entries in the *Annals of Ulster* are records of twelve lunar eclipses and eleven solar eclipses and it is to the subject of eclipses that I now wish to turn. Eclipses, although in some ways a dark topic, throw much light on medieval thinking about the natural and the supernatural. How did people in the Middle Ages explain them and what did eclipses signify? It will be seen that there are more answers than one to these questions.

The physical causes of lunar and solar eclipses had been established in ancient times: a solar eclipse is caused by the moon coming between the sun and the earth and blocking the sun's light (and thus takes place only at the new moon, when the moon's dark side faces earth), whereas a lunar eclipse is caused by the shadow of the earth falling on the moon (and thus takes place only at a full moon, when the moon is facing the sun in line with the earth). This knowledge was transmitted to the Middle Ages

---

[34] Daniel McCarthy and Aidan Breen, "Astronomical Observations in the Irish Annals and their Motivation", *Peritia: Journal of the Medieval Academy of Ireland* 11 (1997), pp. 1–43, quotation at p. 20. The record of the eclipse in the *Annals of Ulster*, s. a. 591/2, recte 594, ed. Seán Mac Airt and Gearóid Mac Niocaill, 1 (Dublin, 1983), p. 94, "is the earliest genuine dated eclipse from the British Isles": D. Justin Schove, *Chronology of Eclipses and Comets AD 1–1000* (Woodbridge, 1984), p. xi, cf. 106–8 (cf. McCarthy and Breen, p. 11).

through various channels and any monk or cleric trained in *computus*, that is, time reckoning, would be familiar with it. Isidore of Seville, the sixth-century encyclopaedist mentioned earlier, whose works were the basic treasuries of knowledge at least to the twelfth or thirteenth centuries, summarized the physical realities of eclipses succinctly: "the moon suffers an eclipse if the shadow of the earth comes between it and the sun"; the sun suffers an eclipse "when the new moon is in line with the sun and obstructs and obscures it".[35]

This astronomical explanation of eclipses was, however, not the only one held in the Middle Ages. Other systems of thought, not based on the physical regularities of orbiting spheres, were also alive. The evidence for these alternative beliefs comes, as is often the case in the medieval period, from the pens of those who opposed them. The sermons of Bishop Maximus of Turin provide a good example.[36] These were composed, probably, around the year 400, and in them, in the manner of the good Christian bishop, he castigates his north Italian congregation for their manifold sins and failings. One of them begins, "You yourselves see, brethren, that my humble self does not cease to labour with care for you and turn you with all haste to good fruits, but the more I labour for you the more I am confounded in you."[37] What have they been doing now, one wonders. Bishop Maximus goes

---

[35] (luna) eclipsim patitur, si inter ipsam et solem umbra terrae interveniat; Eclipsis solis est, quotiens luna trigesima ad eandem lineam, qua sol vehitur, pervenit, eique se obiiciens solem obscurat: Isidore of Seville, *Etymologiae* (as in note 11) 3. 53, 58 (cf. 59).

[36] For the following, see Maximus of Turin, *Sermones* 30–1, ed. Almut Mutzenbecher (Corpus Christianorum, series latina 23, 1962), pp. 117–23 (*Patrologia latina* 57, cols. 483–90).

[37] Et ipsi uidetis, fratres, quod mea non cessat humilitas omni circa uos sollicitudine laborare, et ad frugem bonam uos tota festinatione conuertere; sed quanto plus laboro uobiscum, tanto amplius confundor in uobis: ibid., sermo 30, p. 117.

5. ECLIPSES. Medieval explanations of eclipses were based on exactly the same premises as modern ones: a solar eclipse is caused by the moon coming between the sun and the earth and blocking the sun's light, whereas a lunar eclipse is caused by the shadow of the earth falling on the moon. This was frequently represented in diagrammatic form. What is intriguing about medieval thinking on the subject is that this purely physical explanation did not exclude interpretation of eclipses as also being signs and portents. (London, British Library MS Sloane 2435 (*Image du monde*), fol. 117; French, late thirteenth century.)

on, "For when, a few days ago, I accused many of you of avaricious greed, that same day around evening such a great shouting arose among the people that its irreligious sound penetrated to the heavens. When I inquired what the yelling meant, they said to me that your shouting was meant to help the moon in her travails and assist her with their yells when she was eclipsed."[38] The bishop is outraged: do they think God needs their help to preserve the heavenly lights he has created? And shouldn't they help the moon all the time if they think she needs it? What might happen to the moon when they are asleep? And is it a coincidence that these yelling sessions coincide with drinking sessions? "How, you drunkard," he goes on, "can you see what is happening around the moon in the heavens when you do not see what is going on around you on earth?"[39] He not only scolds, however, but also gives a short and valuable description of the beliefs behind the shouting: these yelling members of his flock are "those who think that the moon can be brought down from the sky by the chants of magicians (*magorum carminibus*)."[40] The idea of an eclipse as a natural occultation was not the only one. Some people believed it resulted from the activities of evil magicians and could somehow be resisted by making loud cries.

Maximus' tirade against the practice of shouting to save the moon during her eclipses is only one example from a loud chorus of educated clerical voices attacking the practice. The early

---

[38] Nam cum ante dies plerosque de uestris auaritiae cupiditate pulsauerim, ipsa die circa uesperum tanta uociferatio populi extitit, ut inreligiositas eius penetraret ad caelum. Quod cum requirerem, quid sibi clamor hic uelit, dixerunt mihi quod laboranti lunae uestra uociferatio subueniret, et defectum eius suis clamoribus adiuuaret: ibid.

[39] Quomodo igitur, ebrius, uidere potes circa lunam quid agatur in caelo, qui circa te non uides quid agatur in terra?: ibid., p. 118.

[40] illos qui putarent lunam de caelo magorum carminibus posse deduci: ibid., sermo 31, p. 121.

medieval penitentials, those finely graded tariffs for a variety of sins, condemn people who cry out "Conquer, moon!" at the time of eclipses and "those who, when the moon is darkened, busy themselves with shouting and witchcraft".[41] Caesarius, bishop of Arles in the first half of the sixth century, rebuked those who "shout when the moon is eclipsed". The moon, he says, "is darkened at certain times by God's command". It is "sacrilegious audacity" to think that one can help her "by shouts or witchcraft".[42] Eligius or Eloi, bishop of Noyon in the seventh century, echoed Caesarius' words when he insisted, "No one, when the moon is darkened, should dare to utter shouts, because, at God's command, it is darkened at certain times".[43] Thietmar of

[41] Si quis "vince luna" clamaverit . . . : F. W. H. Wasserschleben (ed.), *Die Bussordnungen der abendländischen Kirche* (Halle, 1851), p. 422 (Poenitentiale Vindobense a) (cf. pp. 239 (Egbert), 272 (Pseudo-Bede), 598 (Pseudo-Theodore); De illis qui, quando luna obscuratur, clamores suos et maleficia sua exercuerint: Burchard of Worms, *Decretum* 10. 33, *Patrologia latina* 140, cols. 537–1058, at col. 837 (cf. 19. 5, col. 960). The *Indiculus superstitionum* has a clause (no. 21) "De lunae defectione quod dicunt vinceluna", ed. Alfred Boretius, *Monumenta Germaniae Historica, Capitularia regum Francorum* 1 (Hanover, 1883), no. 108, pp. 222–3, at p. 223 (also in Boniface, *Epistulae*, ed. Reinhold Rau (Ausgewählte Quellen zur deutschen Geschichte des Mittelalters 4b, Darmstadt, 1968), pp. 444–8, at p. 446). See Dieter Harmening, *Superstitio: Überlieferungs- und theoriengeschichtliche Untersuchungen zur kirchlich-theologischen Aberglaubensliteratur des Mittelalters* (Berlin, 1979), pp. 250–8.

[42] Et si, quando luna obscuratur, adhuc aliquos clamare cognosctis, et ipsos admonete denuntiantes eis quod grave sibi peccatum faciunt, quando lunam, quae Deo jubente certis temporibus obscuratur, clamoribus suis a maleficiis sacrilego ausu se defensare posse confidunt: Caesarius of Arles, *Sermones* 13, ed. Germain Morin (2 vols., Corpus Christianorum, series latina 103–4, 1953) 1, pp. 67–8 (*Patrologia latina* 39, col. 2239 – Pseudo-Augustine); cf. *sermo* 52, p. 231.

[43] Nullus, si quando luna obscuratur, vociferare praesumat, quia, Deo iubente certis temporibus obscuratur: *Vita Eligii episcopi Noviomagensis* 2. 16, ed. Bruno Krusch, *Monumenta Germaniae Historica, Scriptores rerum Merovingicarum* 4 (Hanover and Leipzig, 1902), pp. 663–741, at p. 707.

Merseburg, a German bishop and chronicler writing in the early eleventh century and referring to a solar eclipse of 990, comments, "but I urge all Christians that they should truly believe that this does not happen on account of some incantation by wicked women nor by eating (*esu*), and it cannot be helped by any action in this world." The true cause of a solar eclipse, he says, citing the late Roman authority Macrobius in his support, is the moon.[44]

Especially interesting are the remarks of one of the great ecclesiastics of the Carolingian period, Hrabanus Maurus. Hrabanus, who taught at the important Frankish monastery of Fulda for many years before becoming archbishop of Mainz from 847 to 856, was interested in the natural world and in time reckoning, on which he wrote a computistical treatise, in which he gives a clear and succinct physical definition of an eclipse.[45] It is a subject that crops up in quite a different way in one of his sermons, which was composed "for preaching to the people" in the early 820s.[46]

---

[44] Sed cunctis persuadeo christicolis, ut veraciter credant, hoc non aliqua malarum incantacione mulierum vel esu fieri vel huic aliquo modo seculariter adiuvari posse, sed sicut Macrobius [1. 15] testatur ceterique sapientes fieri asserunt, id est de luna: Thietmar of Merseburg, *Chronicon* 4. 15, ed. Robert Holtzmann, *Monumenta Germaniae Historica, Scriptores rerum germanicarum*, new series 9 (Berlin, 1935), p. 149; also ed. Werner Trillmich (Ausgewählte Quellen zur deutschen Geschichte des Mittelalters 9, Darmstadt, 1957), p. 130. Thietmar gives the date as 989 but this cannot be correct: Schove, *Chronology of Eclipses* (as in note 34), p. 242.

[45] *De computo* 46, ed. Wesley M. Stevens (Corpus Christianorum, continuatio medievalis 44, 1979), pp. 257–8.

[46] Hrabanus Maurus, *Homilia* 42: "Contra eos qui in lunae defectu clamoribus se fatigabant", *Patrologia latina* 110, cols. 78–80; it has been edited with commentary by Jennifer Clare Woods, "A Critical Edition of Sermons 42–64 from the ninth-century Latin Sermon Collection compiled by Hrabanus Maurus for Archbishop Haistulf of Mainz" (unpublished London Ph.D., 1997), pp. 152–9. She discusses the evidence for dating the collection to 822–5 on pp. 7–8. The phrase "for preaching to the people (*ad praedicandum*

In this Hrabanus describes how one evening he had been sitting contemplating "how he might increase the (people's) profit in the Lord", when "such a great shouting arose among the people that its irreligious sound penetrated to the heavens".[47] The people explain that they are trying to help the moon in its travails. The echo of Bishop Maximus of Turin, writing not in Germany in the ninth century but in Italy in the fifth, will be clear. Medieval authors are always doing this, presenting modern scholars with the question, is all they have written mere literary pastiche? Hrabanus obviously knew Maximus' sermon and proceeds in fact to quote from it more extensively. Yet we can be reassured that he is describing a real personal experience by what he goes on to say, which differs considerably from Maximus' report. Next day, he says, he met some visitors and asked them whether they had noticed anything of this kind. The visitors had actually had an even worse time. During the previous night's eclipse, one had heard the bellowing of warlike horns, another grunting like pigs', yet another had seen people shooting spears and arrows at the moon or scattering the fires from their hearths into the air. The moon, the people had explained, was being attacked by monsters and, unless they brought help, the monsters would devour her. Hrabanus was incensed: such beliefs were demented and insane; there were no such monsters; the people were falling into pagan error. Eclipses, he insists, are the results of "a natural force

---

populo)" occurs in the prefatory letter to Archbishop Haistulf: Hrabanus Maurus, epistola 6, ed. Ernst Dümmler, *Monumenta Germaniae Historica, Epistolae 5 (Karolini aevi 3)* (Berlin, 1899), *Hrabani epistolae*, pp. 379–516, at p. 391 (*Patrologia latina* 110, col. 9).

[47] Nam cum ante dies aliquot quietus domi manerem, et de utilitate vestra, quomodo profectum vestrum in Domino amplificarem, mecum tractarem, subito ipsa die circa vesperam atque initium noctis tanta vociferatio populi exstitit, ut irreligiositas ejus penetraret usque ad coelum: *Patrologia latina* 110, col. 78.

(*naturalis vis*)"; "reason proves"[48] that a solar eclipse is caused by the moon coming between us and the sun and a lunar eclipse by the full moon coming into the earth's shadow.

There was thus a persistent set of beliefs, according to which an eclipse was caused either by the incantations of magicians or by monsters devouring the heavenly bodies. Sometimes these two theories might be combined. One of the German missionaries to the pagan Estonians in the late twelfth century was in danger of his life when his arrival coincided with a solar eclipse: the suspicious native population "said that he was eating the sun".[49] They obviously saw him as a malevolent magician but also regarded an eclipse as a kind of eating or devouring.

The Christian ecclesiastics who condemned such beliefs countered them by a stress on the naturalness of eclipses. Hrabanus talks of "a natural force"; Thietmar refers to Macrobius, the standard science text-book of the early Middle Ages; and one of Thietmar's contemporaries, also a bishop, observing the terror that the solar eclipse of 968 was causing, "was amazed, not at the eclipse of the sun, the cause of which he well knew to be brought about naturally, but at the irrational fear of men".[50]

---

[48] naturalis vis cogit solem ac lunam taliter eclipsin, hoc est defectum, pati. Nam manifesta ratio probat: ibid., col. 79.

[49] Idem frater missus in Estoniam propter eclipsim solis, que in die Iohannis baptiste fuit, a paganis plura passus est vite pericula, dicentibus ipsum solem commedere: Henry of Livonia, *Chronicon Livoniae* 1. 10, ed. Leonid Arbusow and Albert Bauer, *Monumenta Germaniae Historica, Scriptores rerum germanicarum in usum scholarum* 31 (Hanover, 1955), p. 4; also *Ausgewählte Quellen zur deutschen Geschichte des Mittelalters* 24, Darmstadt, 1959, p. 6. The eclipse is that of 23 June 1191.

[50] Stupet super his prudens antistes, non de eglipsi (sic) solis, cuius naturaliter factae optime noverat rationem, sed de irrationabili tot virorum fortium formidine: Anselm, *Gesta episcoporum Leodensium*, ed. R. Köpke, *Monumenta Germaniae Historica, Scriptores* 7 (Hanover, 1846), pp. 189–234, at p. 202; the bishop was Ebrachar of Liège; a later elaboration of this account

Closely linked to this idea of the naturalness of eclipses was the fact of their predictability. If eclipses were caused by the moon coming between the sun and the earth, or the earth coming between the sun and the moon, then, because of the regularity of the rotations of these bodies, it should be possible to foretell when they would be in the right position for an eclipse. The ancient Babylonians had worked out the basic pattern of eclipses, which tend to recur over an eighteen-year cycle, and the Greek philosopher Thales is credited with predicting the solar eclipse of 585 B.C. It is not a simple matter for the amateur, but given the astronomical assumptions, of regularly rotating physical spheres, and some careful mathematics, prediction of eclipses is well within the power of human reason.

Societies that had knowledge of the predictability of eclipses could, indeed, regard that knowledge as a mark of their intellectual, and perhaps general, superiority over societies that did not. The best-known narrative that embodies this idea is not medieval at all but that from the pages of *King Solomon's Mines*, the novel by H. Rider Haggard published in 1885. In this classic "gripping yarn", there comes a moment when the European adventurers who form its heroes are trying to convince a group of African chiefs that they should rise up against the monstrous tyrant Twala.[51] The chiefs ask for a sign, and the narrator, Allan Quatermain, tells how his companion Captain Jack Good rises to the occasion:

> Good went to the little box in which his medicines were, unlocked it, and took out a note-book, in the front of which was an

claims that his views were based on a reading of Pliny, Macrobius and Chalcidius: Reiner, *Vita Evracli*, ed. Wilhelm Arndt, *Monumenta Germaniae Historica, Scriptores* 20 (Hanover, 1868), pp. 561–5, at p. 563.

[51] Chapter 11.

almanack. "Now, look here, you fellows, isn't tomorrow the fourth
of June?"

We had kept a careful note of the days, so were able to answer
that it was.

"Very good; then here we have it—'4 June, total eclipse of the sun
commences at 11.15 Greenwich time, visible in these Islands—
Africa, &c.' There's a sign for you. Tell them that you will darken
the sun tomorrow." . . .

"Suppose the almanack is wrong," suggested Sir Henry to Good,
who was busily employed in working out something on the fly-
leaf of the book.

"I don't see any reason to suppose anything of the sort," was his
answer. "Eclipses always come up to time . . . "

"Well," said Sir Henry, "I suppose we had better risk it."

I acquiesced, though doubtfully, for eclipses are queer cattle to
deal with . . .

Needless to say, the ploy works. At a critical moment Quatermain calls out to Twala's threatening soldiers: "Come but one
pace nearer, and we will put out the sun and plunge the land in
darkness. Ye shall taste of our magic." As the eclipse comes on,
the terrified Africans flee.

The assumptions behind the story scarcely need underlining.
The rational Europeans can use their scientific knowledge to ter-
rify the backward natives. To do so, they use the natives' own
terms – "Ye shall taste of our magic" – in a wholly calculated way.
The dichotomies are science and magic, European and native,
colonist and colonized. It is a story that encapsulates a great deal
and it is not surprising that it crops up on more than one occasion
in modern fiction. In *Prisoners of the Sun*, for instance, originally
published in French in 1949, Tintin uses the trick to free himself,

Captain Haddock and Professor Calculus from a bunch of Incas who have, surprisingly, survived into the twentieth century and are about to sacrifice them.

This colonialist tale has a longer history than one might suspect. Indeed, the gambit was supposedly employed by Christopher Columbus himself, the initiator of European colonization of the New World. Marooned on Jamaica during his fourth voyage of 1502–4, he and his men were dependent on the local native population for food. As time wore on, the inhabitants became unwilling to provide any more food. Columbus, knowing there was a lunar eclipse that night, called together their chiefs, telling them that he had been sent by God, that God was angry with them for refusing to provide the food and that he would demonstrate this by signs in the sky. That night, of course, the eclipse occurred and the natives, overawed, agreed to resume supplying food.[52] Even this, however, is not the earliest case of such a tactic. The trick had been used over four centuries before, in the 1080s, during a campaign of the Byzantine emperor, Alexius Comnenus, against the Pechenegs, a steppe nomad people who had settled in the Balkans. The Pechenegs had sent envoys to Alexius but he was distrustful of them and was seeking an excuse to reject their proposals. At this point one of his secretaries, Nicholas, came to him and informed him that a solar eclipse was imminent. The emperor did not believe him at first, but Nicholas swore on oath that what he said was true. Alexius turned to the Pecheneg envoys and said, "I remit the decision to God". He would, he said, reject their proposals as deceitful "if a sign should soon appear in the heavens". So it happened. Within

---

[52] The account is based on the memoir by Diego Méndez: M. Fernández de Navarette, *Viajes de Colón* (Mexico, 1986), p. 308. It should be noted that Méndez was not an eye-witness at this point, having been sent off to seek help.

two hours, the eclipse occurred, as the moon passed before the face of the sun, in the words of the chronicler recording the incident, in this case Alexius' daughter Anna. She, too, as an educated woman, knew what caused eclipses and could relish the way her wily father used one to fool the barbarians.[53]

The trick employed by these emperors and imperialists, from Alexius Comnenus to Captain Jack Good, was to fool the barbarians and savages by playing on their tendency to see unusual natural events as signs. From the detached and educated Byzantine to the bluff English naval officer in Rider Haggard's tale, the civilized manipulate the primitive by their knowledge of the regularities of nature.

Yet this is far from being the whole story. It is certain, as we have seen, that educated ecclesiastics of the medieval period had access to a purely natural explanation of eclipses and might stress it when confronted with parishioners howling at the moon or talking about monsters eating it. We have heard about Thietmar of Merseburg, emphasising the physical cause of eclipses and even referring to the authority of Macrobius, whose compendium of ancient science was not even written by a Christian. However, closer examination of the context of Thietmar's comments reveals another side to this thinking. He introduces the subject with the following words: "But now as I am going to speak about the death of the empress (Theophanu), I will tell what signs preceded this." Then follows the account of the eclipse. Thietmar is thus both explicit that the eclipse was a sign,

---

[53] Θεῷ τὴν κρίσιν ἀνατίθημι καὶ εἰ μέν τι σημεῖον ἐξ οὐρανοῦ κατὰ ταυτηνὶ τὴν ὥραν ἔκδηλου γένηται: Anna Comnena, *Alexiad* 7. 2. 8–9, ed. B. Leib (3 vols., Paris, 1937–45) 2, pp. 92–3. For an argument that this eclipse is the one of 2 October 1084 rather than that of 1 August 1087, as is generally accepted, see Konradin Ferrari d'Occhieppo, "Zur Identifizierung der Sonnenfinsternis während des Petschenegenkrieges Alexios' I. Komnenos (1084)", *Jahrbuch der österreichischen Byzantinistik* 23 (1974), pp. 179–84.

portending the empress' death, and insistent that it was a natural event, explicable as the moon's blocking of the sun's light.[54]

In fact one common medieval term for an eclipse was "a sign".[55] Just like Twala's soldiers or the Jamaican natives or the Pechenegs, the majority of medieval Christians believed that eclipses meant something. The fact that eclipses had a natural explanation did not mean that they did not also have a pre-dictive function. They were signs as well as regular physical phenomena – predictive as well as predictable.

What were they signs of? It was customary to look up at the skies for a message, but skill was needed in reading it: "The sky is like a book", wrote one twelfth-century poet, "with its pages spread out plainly, containing the future in secret letters".[56] The heavens might be an open book, but you still needed to know the language in which it was written. If eclipses were predictive, then they required interpretation. We can sometimes see medieval writers, especially the chroniclers, grappling with the question of the significance of a given eclipse, and the way they did so is revealing of their assumptions and intellectual instincts. Their

---

[54] On the tension between natural and portentous descriptions of eclipses see Umberto Dall'Olmo, "*Eclypsis naturalis ed eclypsis prodigialis* nelle cronache medioevali", *Organon* 15 (1979), pp. 153–66. For tables showing chroniclers' reactions to eclipses, and other natural phenomena, in the sample periods 1062–1112 and 1215–65, see Isabelle Draelants, "Le temps dans les textes historiographiques du Moyen Âge", in *Le Temps qu'il fait au Moyen Âge: phénomènes atmosphériques dans la littérature, la pensée scientifique et religieuse*, ed. Joëlle Ducos and Claude Thomasset (Paris, 1998), pp. 91–138, at pp. 124–7.

[55] For example, Ralph Glaber's chapter on the solar eclipse of 1033 is headed "De signo quod in sole apparuit": Rodulfus Glaber *Historiarum libri quinque* 4. 9, ed. John France in Glaber's *Opera* (Oxford, 1989), p. 210.

[56] Celum . . . quod quasi librum, porrectis in planum paginis . . . secretis futura litteris continentem: Bernardus Silvestris, *Cosmographia* 2. 1. 3, ed. Peter Dronke (Leiden, 1978), p. 121.

interpretative strategies could be illustrated from any century in the Middle Ages or any place, but, to conclude this chapter, I have chosen three from among the historians of the crusades. An army embarking on holy war was obviously going to be especially sensitive to God's signs.[57]

My first example is from Odo of Deuil's account of the Second Crusade, a fairly disastrous expedition launched in 1147.[58] In the autumn of that year, two Christian armies, one headed by the French king, one by the German, passed through Constantinople on their way to the Holy Land. Relations between crusaders and Byzantines were often tense and suspicious, and this time proved no exception. Louis VII, head of the French army, became involved in complex negotiations with the Byzantine emperor, while the two western armies went on into Asia Minor, the Germans in the lead. At this point, there occurred a partial eclipse of the sun. Odo of Deuil, who was King Louis' chaplain, was with the French army and described its reactions: "When the army saw the sun in the shape of half a loaf, it was fearful that the king had been deprived of some portion of his light by the treachery of the Greeks."[59] So the first impulse of the French soldiers was to fear that their king, back in Constantinople, had somehow been betrayed by the Byzantines. However, adds Odo, another sorrowful thing happened, for at that same time the German army was being attacked and defeated by the Turks. The

---

[57] Cf. Bernard Hamilton, "'God Wills It': Signs of Divine Approval in the Crusade Movement", in *Signs, Wonders, Miracles: Representations of Divine Power in the Life of the Church*, ed. Kate Cooper and Jeremy Gregory (Studies in Church History 41, 2005), pp. 88–98, at pp. 94–8.

[58] Odo of Deuil, *De profectione Ludovici VII in Orientem* 4, ed. Virginia G. Berry (New York, 1948), pp. 82–4.

[59] Cum igitur exercitus...solem in forma dimidii panis...conspiceret, verebatur ne ille...proditione Graecorum aliqua portione sui luminis privaretur: ibid., p. 82.

partial eclipse of the sun thus obviously portended the defeat of one of the two Christian armies. "Because we later learned what it meant," Odo writes, "we have explained the heavenly sign more accurately."[60] The assumptions of Odo and his companions are clear. An eclipse was a sign of some important and usually unfavourable event in the human world. However, its exact signification might become clear only retrospectively, for it is only after the French hear of the German defeat that the sign "can be explained more accurately". Such retroactive interpretation of portents was not uncommon.

My next crusade example is unusual in that an eclipse was regarded as a favourable omen. This was in 1218, when a crusading army landed at Damietta in Egypt. The main chronicler of the expedition, Oliver of Paderborn, has the following to say:

> Soon after the arrival of the Christians there was an almost total eclipse of the moon. Although this very often happens from natural causes at the time of the full moon, nevertheless, since the Saviour says, "there shall be signs in the sun and in the moon", we interpreted this eclipse as unfavourable to the Saracens, as if portending the failure of the ones who ascribe the moon to themselves, placing great weight in the waxing and waning of the moon.[61]

---

[60] Quod postquam didicimus quid significaret, caeleste prodigium rectius exposuimus: ibid., pp. 82–4.

[61] Modico tempore post adventum Christianorum facta fuit eclipsis lune fere generalis, que licet ex causis naturalibus in plenilunio plerumque perveniat, quia tamen Salavator dicit: Erunt signa in sole et luna, hanc eclipsim contra Sarracenos interpretati sumus quasi portendentem ipsorum defectum, qui sibi lunam attribuunt in decremento vel incremento lune magnam vim ponentes: Oliver of Paderborn (or Cologne), *Historia damiatina* 10, ed. Hermann Hoogeweg, *Die Schriften des Kölner Domscholasters . . . Oliverus* (Bibliothek des literarischen Vereins in Stuttgart 202, Tübingen, 1894), pp. 159–282, at p. 178.

The striking thing here (apart from an unusually early association of the moon and Islam, presumably because of the Muslim lunar calendar)[62] is Oliver's explicit acknowledgement that a choice was made to see the eclipse as a sign, even though its natural status was also recognized.[63] Whether he reconsidered the meaning of this eclipse three years later, when he was a prisoner of the Egyptians, we do not know.

My final crusade chronicler is also the earliest of the three. Fulcher of Chartres, who went on the First Crusade of 1096–9 and settled in the east, wrote a *Historia Hierosolymitana* (*Jerusalem History*), which is a very important source for both the First Crusade and the early establishment of the crusader states. In the

---

[62] The idea that the crescent moon is a symbol of Islam originated with Christians, not Muslims. The adoption of the symbol by Muslim states and organizations dates only to the nineteenth and twentieth centuries. See Maxime Rodinson, "La Lune chez les Arabes et dans l'Islam", in *La Lune: Mythes et rites* (Paris, 1962), pp. 151–215, especially p. 203. This means that Bernard Hamilton's idea that the Franks interpreted the lunar eclipse of 11 February 1096 as an auspicious sign "because the moon was traditionally held to symbolize Islam" ("'God Wills It'", as in note 57, p. 95) cannot be correct. An apparent exception in Anna Comnena's *Alexiad* is only apparent. A passage in Book Ten (5. 7) refers to the importance among the Muslims of an ἄστρον. This is translated in Sewter's Penguin Classic as "the moon", with a footnote suggesting "'Moon' should perhaps be supplanted by 'star'", whereas Leib, in the French translation accompanying his edition, renders it as "*astre*" in the main text and gives "*la lune*" in his supplementary notes. Both cite, for further discussion, Buckler's commentary, who, however, is unequivocal that the word refers to the morning star! (Anna Comnena, *Alexiad*, tr. E. R. A. Sewter (Penguin Classics, 1969), p. 310; ed. and tr. Leib (as in note 53) 2, pp. 208 and 244; Georgina Buckler, *Anna Comnena: A Study* (Oxford, 1929), pp. 330–2).

[63] Oliver, the author of the passage, was quite familiar with celestial signs, as his own preaching of the crusade in the Low Countries had been marked by crucifixes appearing in the clouds: J. Van Moolenbroek, "Signs in the Heavens in Groningen and Friesland in 1214: Oliver of Cologne and Crusade Propaganda", *Journal of Medieval History* 13 (1987), pp. 251–72.

course of it, he has occasion to mention a darkening of the moon that took place in June 1113. The moon first appeared red and then black. What was particularly amazing, in Fulcher's view, is that this did not happen on the night of the full moon but on the night before, that is, on the thirteenth rather than the fourteenth day of the month. Now this is physically impossible, and Fulcher's calculations must be wrong, but it leads to an interesting point. "If it had happened on the fourteenth day," he writes, "we would have understood without doubt that it was an eclipse. Therefore because we accepted it as a sign, some conjectured from the redness that blood would be shed in battle, but others predicted from the blackness that a famine would come." Again we see the undetermined nature of eclipse signification. Fulcher himself steps neatly out of the game: "We commit this to the disposition and providence of God, who predicts signs of things to come to his disciples in the sun and moon."[64] Unlike Oliver of Paderborn, who saw the lunar eclipse in 1218 as both natural and portentous, Fulcher seems to be saying that the eclipse he witnessed had to be a sign because it did not meet the natural requirements for an eclipse.

This was, incidentally, standard medieval thinking on the darkening of the sun at the time of the crucifixion. The eclipse of the sun that took place during the crucifixion occurred at the time of the full moon, since this was the feast of Passover. It is physically impossible for a solar eclipse and a full moon to

---

[64] quod si XIV^a die illo esset, eclipsim nimirum eius esse intelligeremus. quod ergo pro signo id accepimus, ex hoc quidam coniectabant rubore in proelio fore fundendum sanguinem; alii vero nigredine significabant venturam famem; nos autem dispositioni et providentiae Dei hoc commisimus, qui in sole et luna discipulis suis praedixit signa fore futura (cf. Luke 21: 25): Fulcher of Chartres, *Historia Hierosolymitana* 2. 61, ed. Heinrich Hagenmeyer (Heidelberg, 1913), pp. 604–5, with a full note explaining the source of Fulcher's error.

coincide because if the moon is between the earth and the sun (which defines a solar eclipse), it cannot also be showing us its full face illuminated by the sun. This was well known in the Middle Ages. Hence, that standard astronomical text-book of the later Middle Ages, Sacrobosco's *Sphere*, when mentioning the eclipse at the crucifixion, states without ambiguity, "that eclipse was not natural but, rather, miraculous and contrary to nature".[65]

There was thus a continuing and fertile tension between the physical explanation of eclipses and their function as signs, as well as a certain open-endedness about what they might be signifying. Classifying an eclipse as natural might be a way of rejecting the belief that it was caused by magicians or monsters, but it did not automatically exclude the possibility that it had a message for human beings below. The machine of this world could also be a book.

The two case studies I have concentrated on here, namely, the debate about the distribution of land and water on the globe and the varying views of the nature of eclipses, show what lively discussion arose from the controversial question of how far purely physical explanations could account for the machine of this world. We have heard scholars arguing that the very

---

[65] illa eclipsis non fuit naturalis, immo miraculosa et contraria nature: John de Sacrobosco, *Tractatus de spera* (as in note 13), p. 117.

---

6. ECLIPSE AT THE CRUCIFIXION The gospels record a darkening of the face of the earth during the crucifixion. Because this coincided with Passover, it must have occurred at the time of the full moon. Because it is physically impossible for a solar eclipse and a full moon to coincide, medieval commentators had to recognize that this eclipse was miraculous. John of Sacrobosco's *Sphere*, for example, states, "that eclipse was not natural but, rather, miraculous and contrary to nature". (Paris, Bibliothèque nationale de France, MS français 2090 (life of St Denis), fol. 34; French, 1317.)

configuration of the globe could be explained only by direct divine intervention, and encountered others whose approach to the question is based solely on natural and physical forces. Some people in the Middle Ages thought an eclipse meant a monster was eating the sun, whereas others regarded it as one spherical body occulting another, although this did not prevent them also regarding it as a portent. Debating in the gardens of a German monastery, observing the noisy rituals of their parishioners, serving as padres in crusading armies, the literate monks and clerics of the Middle Ages, whose task it was to interpret the world, to themselves and to those around them, could draw on a reservoir of inherited naturalistic explanation but did not necessarily find that reservoir fully slaked their thirst.

3

Dogs and Dog-heads

The Inhabitants of the World

I N MY FIRST CHAPTER, I LOOKED AT MEDIEVAL DISCUSSIONS of the boundaries of the supernatural, at the difficult and disputable frontiers between what is natural and what, in varied senses, is not. In the second, my focus was on the physical and material aspects of the universe. In this third chapter, I turn to the inhabitants of the universe, the creatures that lived, or were believed to live, within the machine of the world. I pay particular attention to creatures that seem to have been believed in by many people in the Middle Ages but are not by many people in the modern Western world.

To take one simple example: in his handbook on ecclesiastical services and rituals, the twelfth-century liturgist John Beleth describes the customs practised on St John's Day, 24 June, the old traditional Midsummer Day. Amongst them is the practice of making fires out of animal bones. Beleth gives the rationale for this: "For there are animals called dragons," he writes, "and these animals fly in the air, swim in water and walk on land, and sometimes when in the air they became aroused by lust, whence they often emitted semen into springs and rivers and because of that a deadly year ensued. So a remedy was found for this, that a fire should be made of bones and thus the smoke would drive these animals away".[1] The lighting of these bone-fires (which gives modern English "bonfire") is what Beleth is seeking to explain here; the excited dragons can be taken for granted.

I therefore start my discussion by asking what kinds of creatures were there believed to be. A common and traditional medieval opinion was that there was a tripartite division among sentient beings: "God created three kinds of living spirit: one which is not enclosed in flesh; another which is enclosed in flesh but does not die with the flesh; a third which is enclosed in flesh and dies with the flesh."[2]

The first, living spirits not enclosed in flesh, are the angels; the second, enclosed in flesh but not dying with the flesh, are human beings; the third, enclosed in flesh and dying with the flesh, are the animals (this medieval author had obviously not read James Dickey's poem "The Heaven of Animals", with its assured line "Having no souls, they have come,/ Anyway").[3]

---

[1] Sunt enim animalia, que dracones dicuntur . . . Et ista animalia in aere volant, in aquis natant, per terram ambulant et quandoque in aere concitabantur ad libidinem. Unde sepe spermatizabant in puteis et in aquis fluvialibus, et inde sequebatur letalis annus. Contra hoc ergo inventum est remedium, ut de ossibus fieret rogus, et ita fumus fugaret animalia huiusmodi: John Beleth, *Summa de ecclesiasticis officiis*, ed. Heribert Douteil (2 vols., *Corpus Christianorum, continuatio medievalis* 41–41A, 1976), vol. 41A, p. 267 (*Patrologia latina* 202: 141–2).

[2] Tres quippe vitales spiritus creavit omnipotens Deus: unum qui carne non tegitur; alium qui carne tegitur, sed non cum carne moritur; tertium qui carne tegitur et cum carne moritur: Gregory the Great, *Dialogi* 4. 3, ed. Adalbert de Vogüé (3 vols., Sources chrétiennes 251, 260, 265, 1978–80), vol. 265, pp. 22–4 (*Patrologia latina* 77: 321).

[3] *The Whole Motion: Collected Poems 1945–1992* (Hanover, NH, 1992). For medieval discussion of the fate of animals after the end of the world, see Francesco Santi, "*Utrum Plantae et Bruta Animalia et Corpora Mineralia Remaneant post Finem Mundi*: L'animale eterno", *Micrologus* 4 (1996), pp. 231–64.

The nature of the first category, the angels, was the subject of long and learned debate in the medieval period. Indeed,
such debate provided, in the eyes of later generations, the perfect illustration of the absurd logic-chopping and unfruitful
ratiocination of the medieval schools, for the most notorious
canard about Scholastic thought is from the realm of angelol-
ogy, namely, the supposed debate about how many angels can
dance on the head of a pin. There is no evidence whatever for
such a question being asked in the medieval period, and it seems
that this classic piece of mockery of the abstruse nonsense of
high Scholasticism emerges for the first time in the writings
of the seventeenth-century Cambridge Platonist Henry More,
who, referring to "those unconceivable and ridiculous fancies of
the Schools", mentions discussion of the nature of spirits such
as souls and angels and the question "how many of them booted
and spurred may dance on a needle's point at once".[4] Later the
conceit became quite widely known (a character in one of Addison's plays declares, "Why, a spirit is such a little thing that I
have heard a man, who was a great scholar, say he'll dance ye a
hornpipe upon the point of a needle"), but its general dissemi-
nation seems to be due to its inclusion in the popular *Curiosities
of Literature* compiled by Benjamin Disraeli's father Isaac.[5]

---

[4] *The Immortality of the Soul* (London, 1659) 3. 2, pp. 341–2. I am grateful to
R. James Long of Fairfield University, Connecticut, for the reference. There
is a $5 standing bet for anyone finding any evidence of the question being
asked in the Middle Ages.

[5] Joseph Addison, *The Drummer* (London, 1716), Act 1, Scene I, p. 2; Isaac
Disraeli, *Curiosities of Literature*: the first edition (London, 1791) does not
contain the chapter on "Quodlibets" nor anything on Scholastic debates
about angels, although it does have (p. 38) a short chapter titled "Curious
Scholastic Disquisitions" which cites the question, "whether a hog led to
market by a man on a rope is led to market by the man or by the rope?", an
example of the absurdities of the logicians that had been first presented by
John of Salisbury (*Metalogicon* 1. 3, ed. J. B. Hall and K. S. B. Keats-Rohan

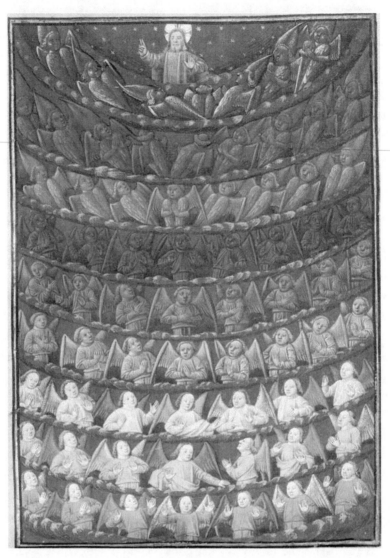

7. ANGELS. One common medieval opinion was that animate creatures fell into three categories: angelic, human, and animal. Angels were distinguished by being "living spirits not enclosed in flesh". This view led to speculation about the precise nature of the angelic body and its relation to physical space, caricatured by the anti-Scholastic thinkers of the early modern period as a debate about how many angels can dance on the head of a pin. This illustrations shows the nine order of angels (Seraphim, Cherubim, and Thrones; Dominations, Virtues, and Powers; Principalities, Archangels, and Angels). (Paris, Bibliothèque nationale de France, MS français 50 (Vincent of Beauvais), fol. 14v; French, 1463.)

Regardless of whether the angels were booted and spurred or were dancing a hornpipe (things rather difficult to reconcile), the nature of the angelic body was in fact a subject of prolonged and thoughtful discussion among medieval theologians. The core of the issue later to be the butt of such derision can be found in a question of Thomas Aquinas: "whether several angels can be in the same place?"[6] Stripped of its bizarre and hostile stage-props of needles and so on, this is the heart of the matter: are angels like material bodies in that one occupying a given space excludes another from occupying that same space?

The question is a profound one about the relationship of being and body and being and space and may perhaps appear less absurd in an age of quantum physics than in that of the billiard-ball universe. Now that scientists are willing to talk of particles or entities that seem to be in more than one place at once or move from one place to another without going through the space between or whose exact location can never be determined, the question of the nature of the angelic body is less quaint.

However, apart from the severely abstract philosophical question, there were important practical consequences that followed

(Corpus Christianorum, continuatio mediaevalis 98, 1991), p. 16). The first edition of Disraeli's work to contain the "angels dancing on a needle" anecdote is the fifth edition (2 vols., London, 1807) 1, p. 99, and it is then included in all the (many) subsequent editions. Disraeli credits "Martin Scriblerus, in Ch. VII" with three quotations about angels – "if angels pass from one extreme to another without going through the middle?", "if angels know things more clearly in a morning?", and "how many angels can dance on the head of a very fine needle without jostling one another?" – but only the first two appear there. See Memoirs of the Extraordinary Life, Works, and Discoveries of Martinus Scriblerus c. 7, ed. Charles Kerby-Miller (New Haven, CT, 1950), p. 123.

[6] utrum plures angeli possint esse in eodem loco: Summa theologiae Iᵃ q. 52 pr., Opera omnia, ed. Roberto Busa (7 vols., Stuttgart-Bad Cannstatt, 1980), 2, p. 262.

from the debate about angelic bodies. For it was generally agreed that what was true of angels was true of both good angels and bad angels, that is, devils and demons: "the devil can influence the physical elements very much through the power of his angelic nature".[7] Hence, conclusions about the angelic body were also conclusions about the power of demons and thus were necessarily significant for medieval demonology and views of witchcraft. In particular, the issue of whether demons could really move things or transform them or have genuine physical contact (notably but not only sexual) was central to the whole history of witchcraft beliefs and witchcraft persecution in the medieval and early modern West.

To take one small aspect of this big topic, what was one to make of the frequent visible manifestations of demons? It was well known that they could transform themselves into angels of light, as St Paul had warned,[8] but they had a thousand tricks up their demonic sleeves. In one short saint's Life, that of Norbert of Xanten, founder of the Premonstratensian Order, who died in 1134, we encounter a demon in the shape of a bear, others who take the form of some mortal enemies of the brethren, one who is embodied as a black lentil on the tongue and a particularly inspired devil who appears to one of the brethren who had a special devotion to the Trinity and, manifesting himself with three heads, claims to be the Trinity. This is not to mention the demon who takes possession of a girl in Nivelles (in the bilingual country south of Brussels) and, "in order to show off his knowledge", not only recites the whole of the Song of Songs

---

[7] operatione diaboli, qui nimirum per angelicae naturae potentiam in elementis mundanis plurimum potest: William of Newburgh, *Historia rerum anglicarum* 3. 6, ed. Richard Howlett, *Chronicles of the Reigns of Stephen, Henry II and Richard I* (4 vols., Rerum Britannicarum Medii Aevi Scriptores, 1884–9) 1–2, at 1, p. 231.

[8] ipse enim Satanas transfigurat se in angelum lucis: 2 Corinthians 11: 14.

in Latin, but then translates it first into French and then into German.[9]

St Norbert understands the nature of these demonic bodies. Confronting the bear, he addresses it: "What do you want, you bloody beast? Your claws are not real, your horrible teeth are wind, your hairy hide is smoke and vapour. . . . Depart with speed!" – and the apparent bear disappears. There is other evidence for good instruction on the nature of demonic bodies in German monasteries in the twelfth and thirteenth centuries. In his *Dialogue of Miracles* of around 1220, the Cistercian monk Caesarius of Heisterbach includes the following dialogue between a novice and his master:

NOVICE: Who can see the devil in is own nature?
MASTER: The physical eye cannot see the devil as he is.
NOVICE: Why?
MASTER: Because the devil is spirit and it is the opinion of almost all the masters that only spirit can see spirit.[10]

So, in some sense, the bears, three-headed apparitions, black lentils, and so forth, are illusory. Yet where did this leave the status of stories of demons' physically transporting people? Could spirits do this, or was it necessary for the spirit somehow to use material form? If so, how?

---

[9] *Vita Norberti* 17, 13, 14, 9, 10, ed. Roger Wilmans, *Monumenta Germaniae Historica, Scriptores* 12 (Hanover, 1856), pp. 670–703, at pp. 692–3, 685, 687, 679, 680; ed. Hatto Kallfelz, *Lebensbeschreibungen einiger Bischöfe des 10.-12. Jahrhunderts* (Ausgewählte Quellen zur deutschen Geschichte des Mittelalters 22, Darmstadt, 1973), pp. 452–540, at pp. 516, 496, 502, 474, 478.

[10] Novicius: . . . quis illum [sc. diabolum] videre posset in sua natura? Monachus: Oculus corporalis diabolum ut est, videre non potest. Novicius: Quare? Monachus: Quia diabolus spiritus est, et spiritum, ut est opinio pene omnium magistrorum, non nisi spiritus videre valet: Caesarius of Heisterbach, *Dialogus miraculorum* 5. 28, ed. J. Strange (2 vols. and index, Cologne, etc., 1851–7), 1, pp. 311–12.

8. THREE-HEADED TRINITY. This highly unusual image shows the Trinity as a three-headed figure. The twelfth-century Life of St Norbert includes an account of a devious devil who appeared to a monk who had a special devotion to the Trinity in just such a three-headed form, tempting the monk to worship him. Because devils were fallen angels, they had (as least originally) the same nature as angels, and there was consequently considerable discussion about their abilities to manifest themselves in physical form or their ability to affect matter. This had practical consequences in theories of witchcraft and in witchcraft prosecutions. (Cambridge, St John's College, MS K.26 (Psalter with Bible pictures), fol. 9v; English?, second half of the thirteenth century.)

In certain circumstance these questions about the nature of demonic agency became particularly pressing. This was when the issue was not simply the powers of demons, for example to manifest themselves in visible form, but also extended to the question how far could demons and humans ally, especially those ill-intentioned humans categorized as witches or evil magicians. William of Auvergne, mentioned in my first chapter, admitted that there was a category "natural magic". Much more common was the belief that magic was demonic. What sort of reality did such demonic magic have?

I touch here on a topic that has been the subject of extensive research by the last few generations of early modern historians of witchcraft, who have worked their way through thousands of court cases, as well as the extensive theoretical literature. Because, in contrast, there is relatively little evidence for actual trials in the medieval period, work on medieval witchcraft has to turn instead to the statements of theologians, the rulings of church councils and other normative and general utterances on witchcraft and magic. I now look at one in particular, to see what common assumptions have been made about it and to point out the difficulties of interpretation that arise. The case in point is the so-called canon *Episcopi*. It is a canon, that is, a decree or ruling of the Church, taking its name, *Episcopi*, from its opening word, as was customary, and it is first recorded around the year 900. Subsequently it was incorporated in collections of canon law of the eleventh and twelfth centuries, including that of Gratian, which became the standard legal handbook of church lawyers for the rest of the Middle Ages, so it was an influential text.

The section of the canon that has attracted most attention is that dealing with

certain wicked women ... who believe that at night, in the company of Diana, goddess of the pagans, and an innumerable multitude of women, they ride on certain beasts, and pass over great distances of the earth in the depth of the night, and obey her commands as their mistress and are summoned to her service on particular nights.[11]

This is, of course, a rather evocative passage. The nocturnal flight of swarms of women, mounted on nameless animals, in the service of their mistress, the goddess Diana, is enough to arouse the hackles of any medieval ecclesiastic, or to enthral certain modern schools of folklorists and feminists. Incidentally, since this canon is first recorded in the Rhineland, it is generally assumed that there must be some German vernacular name lurking behind the classicizing designation "Diana, goddess of the pagans", in all probability *Holda*, "the well disposed one".[12]

What has impressed scholars about this text is the position it adopts on night-flying. Such things, it insists, do not happen in reality. They are *phantasmata*, that is, images impressed on the mind but without physical reality. The devil, by his tricks,

---

[11] quaedam sceleratae mulieres...credunt se et profitentur nocturnis horis cum Diana paganorum Dea et innumera multitudine mulierum equitare super quasdam bestias, et multa terrarum spatia intempestae noctis silentio pertransire, eiusque iussionibus velut dominae obedire, et certis noctibus ad eius servitium evocari: Regino of Prüm, *Libri duo de synodalibus causis et disciplinis ecclesiasticis* 2. 371, ed. Wilfried Hartmann (Darmstadt, 2004), p. 420 (*Patrologia latina* 132: 352). For discussion, see Werner Tschacher, "Der Flug durch die Luft zwischen Illusionstheorie und Realitätsbeweis: Studien zum sogennanten Kanon Episcopi und zum Hexenflug", *Zeitschrift für Rechtsgeschichte, Kanonistische Abteilung* 85 (1999), pp. 225–76.

[12] "Holda" occurs for the first time in Burchard of Worm, *Decretum* 19. 5, *Patrologia latina* 140, cols. 537–1058, at col. 962: daemonum turba in similitudinem mulierum transformatam, quam vulgaris stultitia holdam vocat. For literature, see Tschacher, "Der Flug durch die Luft" (as in previous note), p. 247 n. 69. "*Hold*" means "well disposed" and may well be euphemistic, as in the case of the classical Eumenides and also possibly the high medieval "bonae res" mentioned by Stephen of Bourbon (see note 31).

convinces the women that they are flying in the body, whereas in fact everything happens in the spirit alone. What is worse, not only do the wicked women themselves believe this is happening but belief in the physical reality of night-flying is also widespread amongst the Christian folk as a whole. The danger, in the words of those who drew up the canon, is that people will think "there is something divine or godlike apart from the one God". Priests should therefore explain to their congregations that such flights are only illusory, and the canon concludes by generalizing its point in the ringing words, "therefore, whoever believes that it is possible for any creature to be transformed for better or worse or changed into another species or likeness, except by the creator who made all things and through whom everything was made, is without a doubt an unbeliever."[13]

This text, especially because of its incorporation in the collection assembled by Gratian, has been important both for medieval ecclesiastics, particularly canon lawyers, and for modern scholars of the history of witchcraft.[14] It seems to offer what can be called a sceptical view of the more sensational activities ascribed to witches: night-flying and metamorphosis are illusory, not real. Witches do not fly; human beings do not change into, say, wolves. Indeed, it is contrary to the faith to believe that such things really happen. The author or authors of the canon *Episcopi* are simultaneously making assertions about what is naturally possible and placing bounds on the powers of demons.

[13] cum aliquid divinitatis aut numinis extra unum Deum esse arbitratur. . . . Quisquis ergo aliquid credit posse fieri, aut aliquam creaturam in melius aut deterius immutari aut transformari in aliam speciem vel similitudinem, nisi ab ipso creatore, qui omnia fecit, et per quem omnia facta sunt, procul dubio infidelis est: Regino, *Libri duo* (as in note 11) 2. 371, ed. Hartmann, pp. 420–22 (*Patrologia latina* 132: 352–3).

[14] See the discussion of various medieval authors' attitudes in Henry Charles Lea, *A History of the Inquisition of the Middle Ages* (3 vols., New York, 1888) 3, pp. 493–500.

In the heyday of the witch persecution, 600 years after the canon *Episcopi* was first recorded, considerable efforts were made to explain this ruling away, for the hardliners amongst the witch-hunters, such as the authors of the infamous *Malleus malefi-carum* ("Hammer of Witches") of 1487, pictured the diabolical witchcraft conspiracy that haunted their minds with a grisly literalism. Witches really did copulate with demons, fly through the air to their Sabbats and participate in the gruesome, perverse, and sometimes puerile rituals that took place there. In the words of a recent study of the *Malleus*, "All that the canon *Episcopi* . . . held to be delusions, they found to be the awful truth."[15]

Yet if we look more closely at the canon *Episcopi*, perhaps it is not the bulwark against superstitious paranoia that it might at first appear. The wicked women who are deluded by the belief that they can fly are explicitly described as "perverted by Satan".[16] Their belief that they are physically transported through the air at night is false, but they are genuinely perverted by a real devil.

[15] Hans Peter Broedel, *The Malleus Maleficarum and the Construction of Witchcraft* (Manchester, 2003), p. 114.

[16] The choice of "perverted" is guided by Lea's convincing translation of "retro post Satanam conversae" as "perverted by the devil": Henry Charles Lea, *Materials toward a History of Witchcraft* (3 vols., Philadelphia, 1939), 1, p. 178.

---

9. NIGHT-FLYING. This is probably the earliest depiction of a witch flying a broomstick, although the idea that women might fly at night in the company of devils to hold nocturnal gatherings and harm others was much older. The canon *Episcopi* of c. 900 refers to "certain wicked women . . . who believe that at night, in the company of Diana, goddess of the pagans, and an innumerable multitude of women, they ride on certain beasts, and pass over great distances of the earth in the depth of the night". (Paris, Bibliothèque nationale de France, MS français 12476 (Martin le Franc, *Champion des dames*), fol. 105v; French, 1451.)

Moreover, the opening clause of the canon, which immediately precedes the passage about night-flying, reads as follows:

> Bishops and their officials should strive with all their might to eradicate completely from their diocese the pernicious art of divination or harmful magic, which is an invention of the devil. If they discover a man or woman who is an adherent (*sectator*) of this kind of wickedness, they should expel them from their diocese in shameful disgrace. For the Apostle says, "A man that is a heretic after the first and second admonition reject, knowing that he that is such is subverted".[17] They are subverted, and held prisoner by the devil, who, abandoning their creator, seek help from the devil. And so holy Church should be cleansed from such a disease.[18]

This brief ruling in the canon actually encapsulates a view of witchcraft similar to that elaborated during the great witch-hunt of the early modern period. Harmful magic was invented by the devil and has adherents who have turned from their creator to the devil. It is akin to heresy and is a disease that must be rooted out. The authors of the *Malleus maleficarum* could agree with all of this. It is only on one aspect of the picture – the reality of night-flying – that there is disagreement.[19]

---

[17] Titus 3: 10–11.

[18] Episcopi episcoporumque ministri omnibus viribus elaborare studeant ut perniciosam et a diabolo inventam sortilegam et maleficam artem penitus ex parochiis suis eradant, et si aliquem virum aut feminam huiuscemodi sceleris sectatorem invenerint, turpiter dehonestatum de parochiis suis eiciant. Ait enim apostolus: Hereticum post unam et secundam admonitionem devita, sciens, quia subversus est qui eiusmodi est. Subversi sunt et a diabolo capti tenentur, qui derelicto creatore suo, a diabolo suffragia quaerunt. Et ideo a tali peste mundari debet sancta ecclesia: Regino, *Libri duo* (as in note 11) 2. 371, ed. Hartmann, p. 420 (*Patrologia latina* 132: 352).

[19] Cf. the comments of Russell: "Far from demonstrating scepticism, the canon and its attendant injunctions are important evidence that witch beliefs were

The canon *Episcopi* illustrates the complexities of dealing with normative rulings on harmful magic and, in particular, the tension between the willingness of some churchmen to condemn certain witch-beliefs, such as night-flying and metamorphosis, as contrary to the faith and, on the other hand, their eagerness to prosecute witches and sorcerers who were believed to be really engaged in harmful magic. This point is also illustrated by a less well-known body of material but one which also presents what is apparently a case of early medieval scepticism about the reality of certain kinds of magical or supernatural activity.

Soon after the conversion of the Hungarians to Christianity around the year 1000, their kings began issuing law codes. Stephen, the first Christian king of Hungary, issued two law codes during his reign, and his successors at the end of the eleventh century, Ladislas and Coloman, also issued laws. It is particularly a law of Coloman's that has attracted the attention of historians of witchcraft. This law refers to a particular kind of fearful creature called the *striga*. The term survives in the modern Italian *strega*, which is usually translated either as witch or as or vampire (it also denotes a herbal liqueur), whereas the most common usage of *striga* (with the "i") in the world today is for a devastating parasitic plant, "witchweed". Coloman's law reads, "No inquiries are to be made about *strigae*, which do not exist."[20] It is natural enough to label such a pronouncement as "wholly sceptical".[21] That is, it is wholly sceptical about the existence of *strigae*. This single law of Coloman's has to be put in a wider context, however.

already highly developed in the early Middle Ages", Jeffrey Burton Russell, *Witchcraft in the Middle Ages* (Ithaca, 1972), p. 78.

[20] De strigis vero, que non sunt, ne ulla questio fiat: *Decretum Colomani regis* 57, ed. Janos M. Bak et al., *The Laws of the Medieval Kingdom of Hungary* 1 (Bakersfield, CA, 1989), p. 30.

[21] Russell, *Witchcraft* (as in note 19), p. 97.

First, another law of Coloman's, only three clauses later in his code: "When workers of harmful magic (*malefici*) are discovered, they are to be judged by the envoys of the archdeacon and count."[22] Coloman did not think witchcraft was an illusion, he thought it a punishable offence. It is only about *strigae* that he had his doubts. Second, if we look at Hungarian legislation under Coloman's predecessors, there is a very different view of these *strigae*. In Stephen's first law code, the clauses dealing with *strigae* and with workers of harmful magic (*malefici*) are adjacent in the text. The first reads, "If a *striga* is found, she should, according to the law, be conducted to the church and handed over to the priest for fasting and instruction in the faith." A second offence is to be dealt with by fasting and branding, and, if she offends a third time, she is (rather ominously) "to be handed over to the judges".[23] Harmful magic had even shorter shrift. Anyone daring to overthrow someone's mind or to kill someone through magic was to be handed over to the person harmed or to their relatives – a chilling thought.[24] The Synod of Szabolcs, which met in 1092, also legislated against *strigae*, yoking them together in the same clause as prostitutes (an association that occurs elsewhere).[25]

---

[22] Malefici per nuntium archidiaconi et comitis inventi iudicentur: Decretum Colomani 60, ed. *Laws of Hungary* (as in note 20), p. 30.

[23] Si qua striga inventa fuerit, secundum iudicialem legem ducatur ad ecclesiam et commendetur sacerdoti ad ieiunandum fidemque docendam ... si vero tertio, iudicibus tradatur: *Decreta S. Stephani Regis* 1. 33, ibid., p. 8.

[24] Ibid. 1. 34, p. 8.

[25] *Constitutiones synodi in civitate Zabolch [Ladislai Regis decretorum liber primus]* 34, ibid., p. 60; for a similar association of *strigae* and prostitutes see the provision of the *Pactus legis Salicae* 64 against calling a woman a witch (*stria*) or a whore: *Pactus legis Salicae*, ed. Karl August Eckhardt, *Monumenta Germaniae Historica, Leges nationum Germanicarum* 4/1 (Hanover, 1962), pp. 230–1; cf. *Lex Salica* 96, ed. Karl August Eckhardt, *Monumenta Germaniae Historica, Leges nationum Germanicarum* 4/2 (Hanover, 1969),

Clearly in eleventh-century Hungary there was some debate or confusion (or both) about the *striga*. Was she a human being engaged in wicked activities who needed correction, although she was not identical to the more generic "worker of harmful magic" (*malefica*), or was she simply a superstitious fear, an imaginary terror, and certainly not the object of judicial inquiry? This uncertainty had a long history. For instance, in the eighth century, we can find two Englishmen associated with the Carolingian court, the missionary and martyr St Boniface and the totally obscure Cathwulf, adopting contradictory positions on the *striga*. Boniface, in one of his sermons, on the subject of what is renounced in baptism, gives a long list of the works of the devil that must be repudiated. They include such sins as pride and envy but also concrete evil acts such as killing and adultery and also "consulting diviners, believing in *strigae* or werewolves".[26] Here, just as in the canon *Episcopi*, which dates from about 150 years later, it is the *belief* that is the target of active ecclesiastics, not the practice. Consulting (real) diviners is wrong, but it is believing in

pp. 168–9. Association of witches and prostitutes without the term *striga* is found in the *Capitula Rotomagensia* 6, ed. Rudolf Pokorny, *Monumenta Germaniae Historica, Capitula Episcoporum* 3 (Hanover, 1995), pp. 367–71, at p. 370: De meretricibus a cunctis locis abieciendis et de magicis artibus aruspicum cunctorumque incantatorum seu histrionum penitus delendis. Similar association is made in Anglo-Saxon law: F. L. Attenborough (ed.), *The Laws of the Earliest English Kings* (Cambridge, 1922), p. 108 (Edward and Guthram 11); A. J. Robertson (ed.), *Laws of the Kings of England from Edmund to Henry I* (Cambridge, 1925), p. 92 (Aethelred VI 7).

[26] sortilegos exquirere, strigas et fictos lupos credere: *Sermo* 15, "De abrenuntiatione in baptismate", *Patrologia latina* 89, cols. 870–2 at col. 870. There has been some debate about whether this is genuinely by Boniface. See the summary discussion in Boniface, *Epistulae*, ed. Reinhold Rau (Ausgewählte Quellen zur deutschen Geschichte des Mittelalters 4b, Darmstadt, 1968), pp. 373–4. The passage was transmitted to the eleventh-century Opatovice Homiliary, fol. 171v, *Das Homiliar des Bischofs von Prag*, ed. F. Hecht (Beiträge zur Geschichte Böhmens, Abt. 1, 1, Prague, 1863), p. 66.

(imaginary) *strigae* that is condemned. Contrast this view with that of Cathwulf, an Anglo-Saxon who had moved to the Continent and felt bold enough to write a letter of advice to Charlemagne in the year 775. Amongst the other tasks he sets for this "most godly king" is the rooting out of "workers of harmful magic, those who make magical poisons, those who summon up storms, *strigae*, seeresses, thieves and killers".[27] There is nothing here to suggest any doubt about the reality of these dangerous adversaries of Christian society. The *striga* and the weather-worker are as real as the thief and killer. It is worth stressing that such discordant views could be expressed by those otherwise as similar as Boniface and Cathwulf, both Englishmen under the wings of the early Carolingians. Similarity of background and situation did not necessarily produce common beliefs.

It is, of course, possible, and even likely, that some of this apparent diversity of opinion has purely semantic grounds. Some might have understood *striga* to mean a human being engaged in particular kinds of harmful magic, others a fantastical parasitical creature, for this was certainly one meaning of the word. Let us turn to that viewpoint. The Lombard law code, issued in Italy in 643, prohibited anyone being killed as a *striga*, "because it is not something that Christian minds should in any way believe, nor is it possible, that a woman could eat a man alive from the inside".[28] A century and a half later, Charlemagne's savage rules

---

[27] Maleficos, veneficos, tempestarios, strigas, phitonissas, fures, homicidas . . . : *Epistola 7*, in *Epistolae variorum*, ed. Ernst Dümmler, *Monumenta Germaniae Historica, Epistolae 4 (Karolini aevi 2)* (Hanover, 1895), pp. 501–5, at p. 504. On Cathwulf see Mary Garrison, "Letters to a King and Biblical *exempla*: The Examples of Cathuulf and Clemens Peregrinus", *Early Medieval Europe 7* (1998), pp. 305–28, and Joanna Story, "Cathwulf, Kingship, and the Royal Abbey of Saint-Denis", *Speculum 74* (1999), pp. 1–21.

[28] quod christianis mentibus nullatenus credendum est, nec possibilem ut mulier hominem uiuum intrinsecus possit comedere: *Edictus Rothari 376*,

for the newly conquered and converted Saxons prescribe capital punishment for anyone who, "deceived by the devil", burns a man or a woman because he or she is believed to be a *striga* who eats people.[29] Clearly, these laws are directed against those who accuse other people of being parasitical *strigae*. We have evidence that early in the eleventh century, people also believed they themselves were such creatures, for it was defined as a sin to believe "what many women believe", namely, that while their bodies lay on their beds in the quiet of the night, they travelled through the world with others of their kind, killing Christian men, cooking and eating them, replacing their hearts with straw or wood, and then restoring them to life.[30]

Vigorous debate about the existence of *strigae* and the reality of night-flight persisted throughout the medieval and early modern period. Echoes are found not only in the theological literature but also in the guides to preaching which were produced in large numbers from the thirteenth century onwards. This indicates that their authors had a message about these beliefs that

---

ed. Friedrich Bluhme, *Edictus ceteraeque Langobardorum leges*, *Monumenta Germaniae Historica, Fontes Iuris Germanici Antiqui* 2 (Hanover, 1869), pp. 1–73, at p. 70 (cf. 197–8, ibid., p. 41).

[29] Si quis a diabulo deceptus crediderit secundum morem paganorum, virum aliquem aut feminam strigam esse et homines commedere . . . : *Capitulatio de partibus Saxonie* 6, ed. Alfred Boretius, *Monumenta Germaniae Historica, Capitularia regum Francorum* 1 (Hanover, 1883), no. 26, pp. 68–70, at pp. 68–9.

[30] Credidisti quod multae mulieres retro Satanam conversae credunt et affirmant verum esse, ut credas inquietae noctis silentio cum te collocaveris in lecto tuo, et marito tuo in sinu tuo jacente, te dum corporea sis januis clausis exire posse, et terrarum spacia cum aliis simili errore deceptis pertransire valere, et homines baptizatos, et Christi sanguine redemptos, sine armis visibilibus et interficere, et decoctis carnibus eorum vos comedere, et in loco cordis eorum stramen aut lignum, aut aliquod hujusmodi ponere, et commestis, iterum vivos facere, et inducias vivendi dare?: Burchard, *Decretum* (as in note 12) 19. 5, *Patrologia latina* 140, col. 973.

they wished to convey to a wide lay public. Here, for instance, is a tale from the preacher's handbook written by the Dominican and inquisitor Stephen of Bourbon around 1250. He is discussing the false belief of those women who claim to ride across vast spaces at night in the service of Diana. He says that he has heard of an old woman who, wishing to ingratiate herself with her local priest, went up to him in church and said,

> Master, you should love me dearly, because I have saved your life. For when I was travelling with the "good things" [a well-attested euphemism for night-flyers], in the middle of the night, we entered your house with lamps. I saw that you were sleeping naked and quickly covered you up. Otherwise, if our ladies had seen you naked, they would have had you beaten to death.

The priest enquires how they could have entered his bedroom, which was securely locked, and the woman replies that they can easily enter through closed doors. The priest thereupon draws her into the chancel, locks the door that leads to it and begins to beat the woman with the crucifix. "Get out of here, mistress sorceress!", he says. When she is not able to pass through the door, he lets her go with the message, "Now you see how foolish you are, taking your dreams for reality."[31]

---

[31] Ad hanc ludificacionem, que fit in sompniis, pertinet error illarum mulierum que dicunt se nocturnis horis cum Diana et Herodiade et aliis personis, quas bonas res vocant, ambulare, et super quasdam bestias equitare, et multa terrarum spacia pertransire, et certis noctibus ad dearum servicium evocari... Audivi quod, cum quedam vetula, volens blandiri suo sacerdoti, diceret ei in ecclesia: "Domine, multum debetis me diligere, quia liberavi vos a morte; cum enim ego vaderem cum bonis rebus, media nocte intravimus domum vestram cum luminaribus; ego, videns dormientem et nudum, cooperui vos velociter, ne domine nostre viderent nuditatem vestram, quam si vidissent, ad mortem flagellari vos fecissent." Cumque sacerdos quereret quomodo intraverant domum ejus et cameram, cum ostia essent fortiter serata, ait quod bene intrabant domum januis clausis. Tunc eam invocans

The message of the story was clear: it was ridiculous to believe that people could pass through walls and doors by magic. That message was one that eventually, by the end of the Middle Ages, the inquisitors themselves would ignore.

OUR STARTING POINT FOR THIS DISCUSSION WAS THE TRIPARTITE division of living creatures into the angelic (including demonic), the human and the animal. What if we now turn our attention away from the first category to the other two, humans and beasts? Human beings were animals, there was no doubt about that, but they were animals of a special type, rational animals. According to both ancient and medieval theory, this rationality distinguished humans from animals, and it is this defining feature, rationality, which accounts for the fascination medieval observers felt for any animal activity that seemed to mimic rationality. It was as if brute beasts had strayed close to the line, that indispensable conceptual boundary between human and animal.

Dogs were a prime example, and it is interesting to note that their rational or semi-rational features were usually viewed with admiration and affection. Perhaps this lack of anxiety on the part of observers simply reflects their own security that, however canny dogs might be, humans were unthreatened in their supremacy.

This is summary of canine lore as contained in such generally available texts as encyclopaedias and bestiaries, all drawing on

sacerdos intra cancellam, clauso ostio, verberavit eam cum crucis baculo, dicens: "Exite hinc, domina sortilega." Cum autem non posset, emisit eam sacerdos, [dicens]: "Modo videtis quod fatua estis, que sompnium veritatem creditis": Stephen de Bourbon, *Tractatus de diversis materiis praedicabilibus* 4. 7. 368, ed. A. Lecoy de la Marche, *Anecdotes historiques, légendes et apologues tirés du receuil inédit d'Etienne de Bourbon* (Société de l'Histoire de la France 185, 1877), pp. 323–4.

ancient and early medieval sources:[32] no animal is cleverer than the dog, and its senses are superior to those of the other beasts. The dog alone recognizes its name. More than any other animal, it loves humans and will protect and even die for its master (there was a stock of stories illustrating this point, often augmented). Its sense of smell was particularly remarked, St Ambrose even comparing the "natural erudition" of the dog's scenting power to the syllogistic reasoning of human scholars. "No one will doubt that the dog does not partake in reason," he admits, "but if you consider the power of its senses, you will deem that it enlists the power of reason through the cleverness of its senses."[33] Gerald of Wales, writing centuries later, was equally impressed: "Nature has implanted in its nose all the power of infallible observation."[34] Dogs were thus benignly close to the human/animal line but showed no dangerous tendencies to transgress it. They might sniff syllogistically at the trail of game, could, in the words

---

[32] For example, Bartholomaeus Anglicus, *De proprietatibus rerum* 18. 24–6 (Cologne, 1472 [and many other printings]), fols. 119v–201; *Bestiarium: die Texte der Handschrift MS. Ashmole 1511 der Bodleian Library Oxford in lateinischer und deutscher Sprache*, ed. Franz Unterkircher (Interpretationes ad codices 3, Graz, 1986), fols. 25–9, pp. 52–6. The main sources were Isidore of Seville, *Etymologiae* 12. 2. 25–8, ed. W. M. Lindsay (2 vols., Oxford, 1911), unpaginated (also *Étymologies Livre XII: Des animaux*, ed. Jacques André (Paris, 1986), pp. 111–13); Pliny, *Historia naturalis* 8. 61, ed. H. Rackham et al. (10 vols., Cambridge, MA, 1938–62) 3, pp. 100–6.

[33] Exortem rationis canem esse nemo dubitaverit; tamen si sensus eius vigorem consideres, censes eum sentiendi sagacitate vim sibi rationis adsciscere: Ambrose, *Hexaemeron* 6. 4. 23, ed. C. Schenkl (Corpus scriptorum ecclesiasticorum latinorum 32/1, Vienna, 1897), p. 219 (*Patrologia latina* 14, col. 250).

[34] tanquam totas infallibiles experientiae vires eidem in naribus natura plantaverit: Gerald of Wales (Giraldus Cambrensis), *Descriptio Kambriae* 1. 7, in his *Opera*, ed. J. S. Brewer, J. F. Dimock and G. F. Warner (8 vols., Rerum Britannicarum Medii Aevi Scriptores, 1861–91) 6, pp. 153–227, at p. 71.

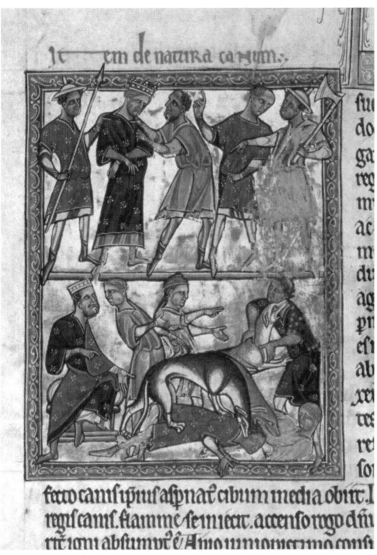

Item — em de natura cannum.

fu(
do
ga
reg
m'
ac
m
du
ag
pri
esi
ab
xri
tœ
re
fo

fecto canıſ ıpıuſ aſpnac abum media obıtt. I
regıſcanıſ. fiamme ſe uıeert. accenſo rogo dın
rū ıam abſumpt ë Amo um ıoruer ıno conſı

10. DOGS PROTECTING THEIR MASTER. Dogs were renowned for their loy-
alty to their master: here the dogs of King Garamantes free him from
captivity. They were admired for other traits as well, such as their ability to recognize their own name and their skill in tracking. St Ambrose
considered that the dog "enlists the power of reason through the cleverness of its senses". Nevertheless, the line between animals and humans
was maintained. Only human beings, it was thought, possessed true reason and immortal souls. (Aberdeen University Library, MS 24 (Aberdeen
Bestiary), fol. 18v; English, c. 1200.)

of one thirteenth-century writer, "smile, as it were, with their tails"[35] and bravely defended their masters to the death, even identifying their murderers by barking, but there was no serious debate about whether they were human or animal. Such debate did take place, however, when it was a matter not of dogs but of dog-heads.

The Middle Ages inherited from the Greeks and Romans the idea that beyond the boundaries of the familiar world there lived types of humans very different from us.[36] They might be gigantic, they might be pygmies. Some had their faces in their chests, others only one eye. They could be threatening, like the cannibals, or appealing, like the people who had no mouths and survived by smelling fruits and flowers. Amongst this diverse range, I wish to turn our attention to the dog-heads, the *cynocephali*, creatures human in form with the exception that they had the heads of dogs.

They were widespread in the medieval period. One is depicted on a Swedish rune-stone of the Viking age,[37] while according to a Welsh poem in the Black Book of Carmarthen, King Arthur himself fought with dog-heads: "On the mountain of Edinburgh/He fought with dog-heads./By the hundred they fell."[38] One version of the story of St Christopher identifies him as a dog-head

[35] cum cauda quasi arridet: Bartholomaeus Anglicus, *De proprietatibus rerum* (as in note 32) 18. 26, fol. 200v (although in the context of deceitful dogs).

[36] John B. Friedman, *The Monstrous Races in Medieval Art and Thought* (Cambridge, MA, 1981) provides an excellent introduction to this subject. The reprint (Syracuse, 2000) contains an updated bibliography. See also Rudolf Wittkower, "Marvels of the East: A Study in the History of Monsters", in *Allegory and the Migration of Symbols* (London, 1977), pp. 45–74.

[37] Birgit Sawyer, *The Viking-Age Rune-Stones* (Oxford, 2000), p. 149, plate 36 (Vg 56).

[38] Tr. Patrick Sims-Williams in Rachel Bromwich, A. O. H. Jarman, and Brynley F. Roberts, eds., *The Arthur of the Welsh: The Arthurian Legend in Medieval Welsh Literature* (Cardiff, 1991), p. 41.

and depictions of this saint in the Eastern Church often show him as literally dog-headed.[39] It is an idea expressed also in the Middle Irish Life of St Christopher in the *Leabhar Breac*: "Now this Christopher was one of the Dog-heads, a race that had the heads of dogs and ate human flesh. He meditated much on God, but at that time he could speak only the language of the Dog-heads."[40]

Clearly, people in the Middle Ages were quite familiar with dogs and also with the human form. Dog-headed people were a radically hybrid notion, which joined in a fashion beyond our experience elements from different areas well within our experience. Moreover, unlike some other hybrids of the imagination, such as, say, the griffin – with an eagle's head and wings and a lion's body – the conception of dog-heads invited speculation about the boundaries of the human and the animal. Just as in the case of modern films and stories about extra-terrestrials, tales about dog-heads posed the question of what is it to be human, or a sentient being, and how far alien form entails alien being. Debate over the limits of a species is still a current scientific issue, while the limits of humanity – who was in and who was out – required repeated definition during the history of European global colonization.

[39] Friedman, *Monstrous Races* (as in note 36), pp. 72–5, with bibliography on pp. 228–9; David Williams, *Deformed Discourse: The Function of the Monster in Mediaeval Thought and Literature* (Montreal, 1996), pp. 286–97, "St Christopher"; Joyce Tally Lionarons, "From Monster to Martyr: The Old English Legend of Saint Christopher", in *Marvels, Monsters, and Miracles: Studies in the Medieval and Early Modern Imaginations*, ed. Timothy S. Jones and David A. Sprunger (Kalamazoo, 2002), pp. 167–82; there is a list of depictions of Christopher as dog-headed in *Lexicon der christliche Ikonographie*, ed. Wolfgang Braunfels (8 vols., Rome, etc., 1968–76) 5, col. 499 (s.n. "Christophorus"); see also the Web site prepared by David Woods of University College Cork: http://www.ucc.ie/milmart/Christopher.html.

[40] "The Passion of St Christopher", ed. and tr. J Fraser, *Revue Celtique* 34 (1913), pp. 307–25, at 309 (Thomas Clancy kindly provided a copy). The *Leabhar Breac* is Dublin, Royal Irish Academy MS 23 P 6.

A document from the mid-ninth century that throws extensive light on just that question is the letter written by Ratramnus,
monk of Corbie, an important monastery in the Somme valley,
to the priest Rimbert.[41] Rimbert was deeply involved in Christian mission work amongst the Scandinavians and the question
on which he consulted Ratramnus is most likely to have arisen
in that context. "You ask", writes Ratramnus, "what you should
believe about the dog-heads, namely whether they are descended
from Adam's stock or whether they have the souls of animals."[42]
The practical implications for a missionary are obvious: if one

[41] Ratramnus of Corbie, *Epistola 12*, in *Epistolae variorum*, ed. Ernst
Dümmler, *Monumenta Germaniae Historica, Epistolae 6* (*Karolini aevi
4*) (Berlin, 1925), pp. 155–7. The letter must date to before 865, when
Rimbert became archbishop of Hamburg-Bremen. There is discussion in
Friedman, *Monstrous Races* (as in note 36), pp. 188–90; Ian Wood, "Chris-
tians and Pagans in Ninth-century Scandinavia", in *The Christianization
of Scandinavia*, ed. Birgit Sawyer, Peter Sawyer, and Ian Wood (Alingsås,
1987), pp. 36–67, at 64–6; and Scott G. Bruce, "Hagiography as Monstrous
Ethnography: A Note on Ratramnus of Corbie's Letter Concerning the
Conversion of the Cynocephali", in *Insignis Sophiae Arcator: Medieval
Latin Studies in Honour of Michael Herren on His 65th Birthday*, ed.
G. Wieland, C. Ruff, and R. G. Arthur (Turnhout, 2006), pp. 45–56.

[42] Quaeritis enim, quid de Cenocephalis credere debeatis, videlicet utrum de
Adae sint styrpe progeniti an bestiarum habent animas: Ratramnus (as in
previous note), p. 155.

11. ST CHRISTOPHER AS DOG-HEAD. Despite the insistence on a sharp
distinction between humans and animals, the idea of hybrids was also
widespread, either in the form of unusual individual births or as distinct
races. One of the more enduring expressions of the latter was the dog-heads
or cynocephali. Medieval writers located them in various distant parts of
the world, debated their nature – especially whether they were human or
not – and, in the eastern (and early Irish) tradition, claimed St Christopher
as one of their number. (Byzantine and Christian Museum, Athens; Greek
icon, 1685.)

encountered dog-heads in Scandinavia, did one preach to them or not?[43] In this pre-Franciscan world, it made no sense to preach to animals, but it was the Christian's duty to win human souls for Christ, however bizarre the body in which the human soul was encased. Ratramnus' advice is revealing. First he asserts that, if the dog-heads are human, then they are certainly descended from Adam – there is no room for the theory of a multiple origin of humanity or the existence of parallel but distinct races of men. He then goes on to list the identifying marks of humanity and finds that the dog-heads do possess them. Given that the shape of their heads and their barking are against them, they nevertheless show many crucial human attributes: they live in villages, practice agriculture, and wear clothes. All these presuppose mastery of technical skill (*ars*) and hence reason, for "knowledge of technical skills is granted only to the rational soul",[44] and it is reason that distinguishes man from the beasts.

[43] Scandinavia was certainly not the most common location in which they were supposedly found, but it did have its proponents. Aethicus, *Cosmographia* 2, ed. Otto Prinz (Quellen zur Geistesgeschichte des Mittelalters 14, Munich, 1993), p. 114, locates *Homines Cenocefalus* in a Baltic island and says they engage in sea-borne trade with the Germans; Adam of Bremen, *Gesta Hammaburgensis ecclesiae pontificum* 4. 19, 25, ed. Werner Trillmich, *Quellen des 9. und 11. Jahrhunderts zur Geschichte der Hamburgischen Kirche und des Reiches* (Ausgewählte Quellen zur deutschen Geschichte des Mittelalters 11, Darmstadt, 1961), pp. 135–503, at pp. 458, 468, places his *cynocephali* in a similar location and describes them as the male offspring of Amazons, who live nearby. On the thirteenth-century Hereford World Map, the *Cinocephales* are depicted on an island close to Norway: Scott D. Westrem (ed.), *The Hereford Map: A Transcription and Translation of the Legends with Commentary* (Terrarum Orbis 1, Turnhout, 2001), map section 4 (facsimile), pp. 186–7 (caption and commentary).

[44] *artis scientia nonnisi rationali conceditur animae*: Ratramnus (as in note 41), p. 156.

Ratramnus' assumptions and his arguments are both worthy of attention. Most of his empirical information about the dog-heads comes from a dossier that Rimbert himself has sent to him. This is how he knows that they live in villages and practice agriculture, including – a point that particularly strikes him – keeping domesticated animals. "I do not see", he writes, "how this could be, if they had an animal and not a rational soul."[45] Rimbert had thus already assembled materials on the subject before submitting his question to Ratramnus. When considering the so-called Carolingian Renaissance, dog-head research must have its small but definite place.

In reaching his verdict on this subject, Ratramnus has clearly had to address the question of what is it that defines humanity. In part, it is a matter of technique and reason, as already mentioned. Yet it is more than that. The dog-heads live in a society, which, despite the contrary authorities, Ratramnus obviously believed does exist. Dog-heads "keep the rules of society" (*societatis iura*). The fact that they live together indicates that they recognize the rule of law. "But", he argues, "there cannot be any law, which common consent has not decreed. But such cannot ever be established or kept without the discipline of morality."[46] A group of moral, rational beings, living in a society bound by laws – this is humanity not mere animality. Moreover, the fact that the dog-heads cover their genitalia is a sign of their decency, which in turn means they have the power of judging between the indecent and the decent, "for no one can blush at indecency

---

[45] Hoc vero fieri posse, si bestialem et non rationalem animam haberent, nequaquam video: ibid., p. 157.

[46] neque ius aliquod potest esse, quod consensus communis non decreverit. Verum talem praeter moralitatis disciplinam nec constitui nec custodiri aliquando potuit: ibid., p. 155.

unless they have a certain recognition of decency".[47] This moral discrimination also shows their rationality, just as much as their ability to build and plough and weave does.

Ratramnus does cite earlier authorities to support his views, relying heavily on Augustine, referring to the discussion of monstrous races in the encyclopaedist Isidore of Seville and mentioning the story of St Christopher, who "is known to have been of this race of men",[48] but his primary goal in this letter is to set out his criteria of humanity and to measure against them the known facts about the dog-heads.

If this intriguing letter did arise in response to problems of the mission field, it was certainly not the last time that dog-heads and evangelization came together. The Christian mission, as defined in Christ's words in the New Testament, was "to preach the gospel to every creature in the whole world",[49] and those creatures included dog-heads if there were any and if they were human. Hence the great twelfth-century tympanum of the abbey church of Vézelay in Burgundy, which depicts Christ charging his disciples to preach "to the ends of the earth",[50] shows a variety of races, including the pygmies, using ladders to mount their horses, the Panotii, with ears so huge they can use them as blankets, and, of course, the dog-heads.[51] The same association of these exotic distant people and the universal Christian message is found in a series of illustrations of Pentecost in several Byzantine and Armenian Psalters and Gospel Books, where

---

[47] Erubescere namque nemo potest de turpitudine, nisi cui contigit quaedam honestatis cognitio: ibid., p. 156.

[48] hoc de genere hominum fuisse cognoscitur: ibid.

[49] Mark 16: 15.   [50] Acts 1: 8.

[51] The sculptures have been frequently reproduced. See, for instance, Véronique Rouchon Mouilleron, Vézelay: The Great Romanesque Church (Eng. tr., New York, 1999), pp. 43 (general context of dog-heads), 49 (detail). Also Friedman, Monstrous Races (as in note 36), p. 81, fig. 29e.

dog-heads appear among the international crowd that characterized the occasion.[52]

If a voice was sometimes heard locating the dog-heads in Scandinavia, the more common opinion by far was that they lived
in "the East"- that vast, amorphous, opulent, unknown region
which occupied not so much a portion of the globe as a space
in the imagination of Westerners. Yet the east was not always
and only fantasy, for one of the most important developments
of the period 1050–1300 was the enormous increase in Western contact with the east and knowledge of it. Some of this was
warlike. The crusades, launched in 1095, produced something
like Western colonies in Syria and Palestine. Vézelay, with its
message of mission, was also a focal point for this more violent
form of Christian expansion: St Bernard preached the Second
Crusade there, and it was the muster point for the armies of the
Third Crusade. At the same time as crusaders penetrated to new
parts of the Mediterranean and Middle East, traders, especially
Italian merchants, made their way even further into Asia, while
in the thirteenth century a wholly new situation was created for
East-West contact by the conquests of the Mongols. Although
frightening and destructive, Mongol armies eventually created
an empire that stretched from Korea to Persia and from the borders of Poland to the borders of Vietnam, a new Great Power
that made dealings across its vast extent easier than ever before.
Moreover, from the point of view of Western Christians, there
was the advantage that the Mongols were not initially Muslim

---

[52] For instance the Pentecost scenes in the Gospel Book of T'oros Roslin of
1262 (Baltimore, Walters Art Gallery MS 539), fol. 379, and MS Erevan,
Matenadaran 10675 of 1268, fol. 305 (312), both reproduced in Sirarpie Der
Nersessian, *Miniature Painting in the Armenian Kingdom of Cilicia from
the Twelfth to the Fourteenth Century* (Dumbarton Oaks Studies 31, 2 vols.,
1993), 2, figs. 217–18, with discussion at 1, pp. 41–2 and 62.

and relied extensively on Asian Christians, mostly Nestorians, as advisers and administrators. There was even for some time the dream that the Khans themselves might convert to Christianity.

In this new situation, with a trans-Asiatic empire with possible Christian sympathies, Western Christians probed more deeply into Asia and wrote more observantly about it than ever before. Now, if ever, was the time to make contact with the dog-heads. Amongst the emissaries sent to the Mongols in the mid-thirteenth century was the Franciscan friar William of Rubruck, who left Constantinople in the spring of 1253, spent three or four months at the Mongol capital of Karakorum in 1254, and returned to the crusading states in the spring of 1255, two years after his journey had begun. William is an alert and sympathetic figure, who describes his adventures and the peoples he met with precision.[53] His initial horror at drinking *cosmos*, the fermented mare's milk of the steppe nomads, is vividly described – "at the first draught I sweated all over because of it horror and unfamiliarity" – as also is his swift reconciliation with it.[54] As an ethnographic observer of diet, costume, burial customs, hair-styles, and on so, he is of the first importance.

There was one category of exotic people he never met, however. While at Karakorum, as he himself relates, "I asked about the monsters or monstrous humans that Isidore and Solinus tell about [Isidore is the encyclopaedist Isidore of Seville and

[53] William of Rubruck, *Itinerarium*, ed. Anastasius van den Wyngaert, *Sinica Franciscana I: Itinera et Relationes fratrum minorum saec. XIII et XIV* (Quaracchi, 1929), pp. 164–332. There are English translations in Christopher Dawson (ed.), *The Mongol Mission* (London, 1955), repr. as *Mission to Asia* (Toronto, etc., 1980), pp. 87–220, and in *The Mission of Friar William of Rubruck*, ed. Peter Jackson and David Morgan (Hakluyt Society, 2nd Ser., 173, 1990).

[54] ad cuius haustum totus sudavi propter orrorem et novitatem, quia nunquam biberam de eo: ibid. 9, p. 189.

Solinus the third-century abbreviator of Pliny]. They said to me that they had never seen such beings, wherefore we wondered very much whether it were true."[55] The great encyclopaedias and standard texts of the late Roman and early medieval world, which had furnished the minds of generations of western monks and clerics, were now, perhaps rather surprisingly, being put to the test in Mongolia – put to the test and found wanting. Westerners found that even their most familiar exotics, the pygmies, monopods, and dog-heads they had been brought upon might not survive real confrontation with the unfamiliar world. As they found the east full of new experiences, they might simultaneously have to forgo some of their old assumptions about it. Acquiring a taste for fermented mare's milk and becoming sceptical of the existence of dog-heads were both part of the education of this Flemish friar in distant lands.

William of Rubruck's doubts and dilemmas are echoed by another Franciscan traveller in Asia of a later generation, John de Marignollis, who was sent east by the pope in the 1330s, spent many years in China encouraging the convert community there and eventually returned by way of India, where he also spent a prolonged period.[56] There he, too, hunted for the monstrous

---

[55] Quesivi de monstris sive de monstruosis hominibus de quibus narrat Ysidorus et Solinus. Ipsi dicebant michi quod nunquam viderant talia, de quo multum miramur si verum sit: ibid. 29, p. 269.

[56] After his return to Europe John became court chaplain to Charles IV, Holy Roman Emperor and king of Bohemia. This explains the curious fact that the reminiscences of his travels are to be found in the history of Bohemia he wrote in the 1350s: *Iohannis de Marignolis Chronicon Bohemorum*, ed. J. Emler, *Fontes Rerum Bohemicarum* 3 (Prague, 1882), pp. 492–604. The sections relevant to Asia were reprinted by van den Wyngaert, *Sinica Franciscana I* (as in note 53), pp. 524–60. There is an English translation of the Asian sections, with commentary, in Henry Yule, *Cathay and the Way Thither* 3, 2nd ed., rev. Henri Cordier (Hakluyt Soc., 2nd Ser., 37, 1914), pp. 175–269.

12. MONOPOD. The idea of exotic peoples living in "the East" was an ancient one, going back to Pliny and beyond. They might be giants or pygmies, have only one eye, or have faces in their chests. Amongst them were the monopods, people with one huge foot that, lying on their backs, they could use as an umbrella. As European knowledge of Asia opened up

races described in the old literature – the one-eyed people, the
hermaphrodites, the dog-heads, the people with one huge foot
that, lying on their backs, they could use as an umbrella. "I
travelled through all the provinces of India with great curiosity," John writes, adding with a pious flourish "for my mind
was often more full of curiosity than virtue". Yet it seems that
it was his curiosity on which he prided himself: "I wished to
know everything if I could, and I put more effort than any
other who is read of or heard of, into investigating the wonders of the world." Despite his wide travels and enquiries, especially where merchants congregated, his efforts were in vain.
"Never was I able to track down such peoples in the world
in reality; instead, people asked *me* whether there were such
creatures."[57]

[57] Ego tamen omnium provinciarum Yndorum curiosissimus peragrator, sicut
sepe plus habui animum curiosum quam virtuosum, volens omnia nosse,
si possem, et qui plus dedi operam, ut puto, quam alius, qui legatur vel
sciatur, ad investigandum mirabilia mundi et transivi per principaliores
mundi provincias, maxime, ubi tocius orbis mercatores conveniunt, scilicet in insula dicta Ormes; nunquam potui investigare pro vero tales gentes
esse in mundo; ymo ipsi a me petebant, utrum essent. Nec est aliqua nacio
talis, nisi ut dixi monstrum, nec illi, qui finguntur uno pede sibi umbram
facere, sunt nacio una, sed quia omnes Yndi communiter nudi vadunt, por-
tant in arundine parvum papilionem semper in manu, quem vocant cyatyr,
sicut ego habeo Florencie, et extendunt contra solem et pluviam, quando vol-
unt. Istud poete finxerunt pedem: ed. Emler, p. 509; ed. Van den Wyngaert,
pp. 545–6.

12 (*continued*) in the thirteenth and fourteenth centuries, the merchants
and missionaries who travelled in China and India were somewhat bemused
not to encounter these people. One Italian friar thought the idea of
monopods might have arisen from a mistaken report of the Indians carrying their characteristic umbrellas. (London, Westminster Abbey Library,
MS 22 (Bestiary), fol. 1v; English, late thirteenth century.)

"There is no such nation", concluded John, but his native ingenuity was not willing to rest with this simple conclusion. What
of those people who were supposed to have one enormous foot,
which, lying on their backs, they could use as an umbrella? What
lies behind this, says John, is that the Indians all carry umbrellas
("just like the one I have in Florence", he adds) and that these,
when extended above their heads, might give rise to the idea
that they had an enormous single foot sheltering them against
sun and rain. As a rationalistic and naturalistic explanation it
is no cruder than any such attempt to explain the fantastic or
legendary as misunderstood realities.

John de Marignollis' experiences underline the simple but
important point that monsters are always elsewhere. His vora-
cious search for dog-heads and other human anomalies extended
as far as India, but there the response seems to have been, "we
thought they lived where *you* came from". The term "the Other"
(capitalized) has indeed become rather a tired one, but it is hard
to find any more appropriate label for this tendency to project
the fantastic, the scarcely imaginable and the extraordinary into
distant locales. John de Marignollis' India was his Other, but
when he got there he found he was theirs.

I WISH TO CONCLUDE THIS CHAPTER WITH A FEW GENERAL REF-
lections that must be based on a working premise. The premise
is that most people reading this book believe in the existence
neither of female creatures who go around at night replacing
men's hearts with hearts of straw nor in dog-headed people in
India or anywhere else. This premise will enable me to use that
dangerous pronoun "we" freely. So I can now pose the question,
what do "we" do about beliefs "we" do not share? This is a
problem faced by all historians, but a similar one is encountered
by many social scientists and others, notably anthropologists

dealing with societies not their own. They face the question, what kind of explanation do alien beliefs require, just as historians have to confront the same issue when it comes to past beliefs we do not share.

In particular, historians must raise the difficult question, even if they cannot answer it, of whether past beliefs we think false require different kinds of explanation and interpretation from past beliefs we think true. For instance, Isaac Newton, the scientist who discovered the laws of gravity, also accepted the truth of biblical prophecies and alchemy. If we believe in gravity but not in alchemy (vice versa would do just as well, of course), do we need to approach analysis of Newton's thinking on the two topics in different ways? Newton himself said, "A man may imagine things that are false, but he can only understand things that are true."[58] When writing the *Principia* was he then "understanding", but when he studied the transmutation of metals, was he then only "imagining"?

Most of the topics I have been discussing in this chapter could reasonably be classed as products of the imagination – not only in the medieval sense of imagination, namely, the faculty of the soul which apprehends things that are absent,[59] but also in one of its most common modern senses, namely, the power of the human mind to produce imaginary things. Yet we should beware

---

[58] *Sir Isaac Newton's Theological Manuscripts*, ed. Herbert McLachlan (Liverpool, 1950), p. 17, cited in Michael White, *Isaac Newton: The Last Sorcerer* (London, 1997), p. 5.

[59] Ymaginacio qua anima intuetur formas rerum corporalium cum sunt absentes: Bartholomaeus Anglicus, *De proprietatibus rerum* (as in note 32) 3. 6, fol. 10. In general see Harry A. Wolfson, "The Internal Senses in Latin, Arabic and Hebrew Philosophic Texts", *Harvard Theological Review* 28 (1935), pp. 69–133, and E. Ruth Harvey, *The Inward Wits: Psychological Theory in the Middle Ages and the Renaissance* (Warburg Institute Surveys 6, London, 1975).

of a premature categorization. We may believe in the existence neither of *strigae*, the nocturnal, blood-sucking, heart-removing women, nor of dog-heads, tending their crops and covering their genitals, but it is worth pointing out that we have not really created a category of being simply by a common lack of belief on our part. "Things we don't believe in" is certainly a subjective category for us but corresponds poorly, if at all, to a class of objects in the world. For those who did believe, to believe in a *striga* and to believe in a dog-head were different. The latter were not seen in the normal course of things, because they lived far away, in the distant North or the exotic East – this is why they appear so frequently on the margins of medieval world maps. If they existed, they were certainly natural and, most would agree, human. Yet in addition to such creatures, tangible but distant, there were other beings who lived within one's own society but were not usually identifiable by the ordinary senses – *strigae*, witches, demons. They were either not ordinarily visible, as in the case of demons or the *striga* conceived of as a non-human predatress, or, in the case of the witch or witch-type *striga*, they were visible only in the apparently innocuous shape of our human neighbours.

Travel can dispel beliefs in strange faraway creatures, as we have seen in the case of the Franciscans in Asia, who came to doubt the reality of dog-heads and the rest as they ventured to Mongolia and India in the thirteenth and fourteenth centuries. The process continued as Europeans expanded throughout the globe in the modern period. Slowly the imaginary geographic spaces where hybrids, monsters, and marvels could be located contracted. As European imperialism reached its crescendo in the late nineteenth and early twentieth century, such regions became more and more limited. Rider Haggard situated *King Solomon's Mines* in unknown central Africa, Conan Doyle's *Lost World* of 1912 is deep in the Amazonian jungle, and the Shangri-La of *Lost Horizon* (the place that launched a thousand bungalow names, in the novel published in 1933 and filmed in 1937) occupies a valley high in the mountains of central Asia.[60] It has been pointed out that it was only to be a matter of time before realms of the imagination would have to be located beyond the earth altogether, as the genre of science fiction took up the baton.[61]

So, as European culture expanded, becoming familiar with this sphere of earth and water we inhabit, it pushed enchanted Lost Worlds into Tibet or the Matto Grosso. It did not, however, simultaneously free itself from its own demons. The ships that carried Europeans to the New World brought Satan with them. To cite only one of the most notorious cases, the Salem witchcraft trials show that, in a New England without a dog-head in sight, demons flourished. Inner monsters are harder to deal with than outer monsters.

We have seen that there were people who believed in *strigae* and people who did not, people who believed in dog-heads and those who came not to. I do not wish to labour the point I have already made, that the medieval period witnessed great diversity of belief in the sphere of the natural and the supernatural. In this chapter, however, I have been concentrating on creatures that, in general terms, we no longer believe in – dragons, witches, dog-heads. I would not wish to give them a greater prominence in the overall picture of the Middle Ages than they should have, so I conclude with a quotation that illustrates how quite different attitudes might be widely held. It comes from the worried pen of an Augustinian prior in the heart of the medieval Catholic

---

[60] H. Rider Haggard, *King Solomon's Mines* (London, 1885), Arthur Conan Doyle, *The Lost World* (London and New York, 1912), James Hilton, *Lost Horizon* (London, 1933).

[61] C. S. Lewis, "On Science Fiction", in *Of Other Worlds* (London, 1966), pp. 59–73, at pp. 67–8.

world, England around the year 1200: "There are many people who consider only what they can see and do not believe there are good and bad angels nor that the soul of man lives on after the death of the body nor that there are any other spiritual and invisible things."[62]

These were presumably the people who believed in needles but not in angels dancing on them.

[62] Multique sint qui, solum ea que vident pensantes, nec bonos angelos sive malos esse, nec animam hominis post mortem corporis vivere, nec alia spiritualia et invisibilia esse credant: Peter of Cornwall, *Liber revelationum,* Lambeth Palace MS 51, fol. 2.

4

"The Secrets of Nature and Art"

Roger Bacon's Opus maius

T HE TROUBLE WITH CONTEMPORARY WESTERN EDUCA-
tion is that far too little emphasis is placed on science, mathematics, and foreign languages, which are the essential
foundations of research and have direct practical benefits. Experimental science can lead to all sorts of technical breakthroughs
and mathematics is the gateway to science. Foreign languages
are essential for trade and diplomacy. Especially now, when relations with the Muslim world are so crucial, it is a disgrace that
there are so few diplomats trained in the Arabic language.

These are the views of Roger Bacon, writing in 1267.

In my final chapter, I take a rather different approach from that
in the first three. In those, I selected an issue – the definition of
the supernatural, the nature of eclipses, the existence of dog-
heads – and looked at debate across the medieval period, taking
my examples in a cavalier fashion from many centuries, as long
as I thought they could enlighten the topic. Here, I instead con-
centrate on one individual, a thinker from the thirteenth century.
I believe his thought intersects with many of the themes already
discussed and can serve to show how these strands might inter-
weave in the intellectual life of one man. Whether we should
classify his views under the natural or the supernatural heading
of these chapters is an open and debatable question. The man is
Roger Bacon, an English-born Franciscan friar, seen by some as a

"precursor of modern science" but also famously mythologized as Friar Bacon the magician.[1]

Little is known about Bacon's life. Given the nature of medieval documentation, it is not surprising that we cannot establish when or where he was born and when or where he died, but, beyond that common uncertainty, there is little sure fact about the dates and locations of his teaching career or of his entry into the Franciscan Order, not to mention scholarly disagreement about whether one important event, his imprisonment by the Order, actually took place at all.[2] It is certain that he studied and taught at Oxford and Paris, the two most important universities north of the Alps, and that his scholarly career extended from at least the 1240s to the 1290s,[3] but rather than

---

[1] "Precursor of modern science": a phrase used by George Molland, "Bacon, Roger (c.1214–1292?)", *Oxford Dictionary of National Biography* (Oxford, 2004) vol. 3, pp. 176–81, at p. 178, with consideration of the validity of such a description; he also provides an introduction to Bacon's legendary reputation in "Roger Bacon as Magician", *Traditio* 30 (1974), pp. 445–60. The most important source for the legend is the sixteenth-century romance *The Famous Historie of Fryer Bacon* (London, 1627). Bacon's posthumous reputation receives detailed treatment in Amanda Power, "A Mirror for Every Age: The Reputation of Roger Bacon", *English Historical Review* 121 (2006), pp. 657–92.

[2] For a sceptical view, see, for example, Lynn Thorndike, *A History of Magic and Experimental Science during the First Thirteen Centuries of Our Era* (2 vols., New York, 1923) 2, pp. 628–9. The evidence for his imprisonment is discussed later in the chapter.

[3] The date of the 1240s is established by the fact that Bacon had seen the Parisian scholar Alexander of Hales (d. 1245) and twice heard William of Auvergne, bishop of Paris (d. 1249), disputing: *Opus minus*, ed. Brewer (as in following note), pp. 325–6, with discussion and correction to the text in A. G. Little (ed.), *Roger Bacon: Essays Contributed by Various Writers on the Occasion of the Commemoration of the Seventh Centenary of His Birth* (Oxford, 1914), pp. 8–9 n. 9; *Opus tertium* 23, ed. Brewer (as in following note), p. 74. That of the 1290s is based on the reference in Bacon's *Compendium studii theologiae* (1. 2) to "hunc annum Domini 1292^{m}", ed.

trying to augment this ghostly outline, I begin my discussion of Bacon with something big, incontrovertible, and closely datable, namely, the trio of works he wrote in the year 1267. This was his *annus mirabilis*, and if all his other writings had perished, the three works of that time – the *Opus maius*, *Opus minus*, and *Opus tertium* (i.e., "Bigger Work", "Littler Work", and "Third Work") – would ensure him a place as one of the most interesting thinkers of the thirteenth century.[4]

H. Rashdall (British Society of Franciscan Studies 3, 1911), p. 34, ed. and tr. Thomas S. Maloney (Leiden, 1988), p. 46.

[4] Editions: Roger Bacon, *Opus maius*, ed. J. H. Bridges (3 vols., London, 1900) – the three-volume edition consists of a reprint of the two volumes published at Oxford in 1897 plus a volume in which parts 1–3 of the *Opus* are re-edited, along with numerous corrigenda. Part 7, on moral philosophy, has been edited from the very manuscript Bacon sent to the pope: Roger Bacon, *Moralis philosophia*, ed. Eugenio Massa (Zurich, 1953). See also K. M. Fredborg, L. Nielsen and J. Pinborg, "An Unedited Part of Roger Bacon's Opus maius: *De signis*", *Traditio* 34 (1978), pp. 75–136. The accompanying letter to the pope is printed in "An Unpublished Fragment of a Work by Roger Bacon", ed. F. L. Gasquet, *English Historical Review* 12 (1897), pp. 494–517. There is a translation of the *Opus maius* which I have generally used for my citations, although occasionally adapting it: *The Opus Majus of Roger Bacon*, tr. Robert Belle Burke (2 vols., Philadelphia, 1928, paginated continuously). (I have given references to Burke's translation even when I have not used it or have adapted it.)

An incomplete text of the *Opus minus* was edited by J. S. Brewer, in *Fr. Rogeri Bacon opera quaedam hactenus inedita* 1 (Rerum Britannicarum Medii Aevi Scriptores, 1859) pp. 313–89 (no more volumes were published). Part of it was also printed by Bridges as the conclusion of Part Four of the *Opus maius* (above) 1, pp. 376–403.

Chapter 1–75 of the *Opus tertium* were edited by Brewer, *Fr. Rogeri Bacon opera* (above), pp. 1–310. See also *Un Fragment inédit de L'Opus tertium*, ed. Pierre Duhem (Quaracchi, 1909); *Part of the 'Opus tertium' of Roger Bacon*, ed. A. G. Little (Aberdeen, 1912).

The date of 1267 is given explicitly in the *Opus maius* 4, ed. Bridges 1, pp. 280–1, tr. Burke, p. 302, and the *Opus tertium* 69, ed. Brewer, p. 278.

The bibliography on Roger Bacon is large. For guidance, see F. Alessio,

Fortunately we know exactly the circumstances that stimulated Bacon to write these three works. At some point there
had been contact, perhaps indirect, between Bacon and Guy
Foulquois, who was, from 1261, a cardinal and also the legate
deputed, unsuccessfully, to settle the conflict between Henry III
of England and dissident barons led by Simon de Montfort.[5]
Bacon had apparently enthused about a work of his to Guy and
the cardinal had naturally assumed it was a work Bacon had
already written. Unfortunately, in the manner of enthusiastic
writers and scholars of all generations, Bacon had actually only
had the idea for the book. This made it rather awkward when,
in 1264, Guy became pope, as Clement IV, and wrote to Bacon
commanding him to send a fair copy of the work they had discussed. Bacon, however, rose to the occasion, and indeed sur-
passed requirements. Not only did he produce the *Opus maius*
(of well over a quarter a million words), but, because he was
nervous that this might be lost in transmission, or too long or
(paradoxically) incomplete, he then proceeded to produce the

"Un secolo di studi su Ruggero Bacon (1848–1957)", *Rivista critica di storia della filosofia* 14 (1959), pp. 81–102; Jeremiah Hackett and Thomas S.
Maloney, "A Roger Bacon Bibliography (1957–1985)", *New Scholasticism*
61 (1987), pp. 184–207; Thomas S. Maloney, "A Roger Bacon Bibliography
(1985–1995)", in *Roger Bacon and the Sciences: Commemorative Essays*,
ed. Jeremiah Hackett (Studien und Texte zur Geistesgeschichte des Mittelalters 57, Leiden, 1997), pp. 395–403. See also Suzannah Biernoff, *Sight and
Embodiment in the Middle Ages* (Basingstoke, 2002), pp. 73–107; Jeremiah
Hackett, "Roger Bacon", in *A Companion to Philosophy in the Middle Ages*,
ed. Jorge J. E. Gracia and Timothy B. Noone (Malden, MA, and Oxford,
2003), pp. 616–25.

[5] Guy's career to 1265 is discussed in Joseph Heidemann, *Papst Clemens IV:
Das Vorleben des Papstes und sein Legationsregister* (Kirchengeschichtliche
Studien 6/4, Münster, 1903), with an edition of his letters regarding the
dispute between Henry and his barons at pp. 194–248. His negotiations
in summer 1264 are summarized in John Maddicott, *Simon de Montfort*
(Cambridge, 1994), pp. 291–306.

Opus minus as a safeguard, guide, and supplement. From the same motives, he completed his trio with the *Opus tertium* (300 printed pages in the standard edition), which he describes as serving "the understanding and perfecting of both the preceding works".[6]

The word "works" has a peculiar complexity when we consider Bacon, for one feature of his mature years was his incessant urge to repeat himself, to cross-reference his writings but also to revise them and, it seems, rename them. This repetition and overlap and his apparently constantly changing conception of his overall "principal work" mean that scholars have not succeeded either in producing a definitive edition of his works or in agreeing what should go into such an edition if it were to be produced. This fussing and fretting side of Bacon's creative impulse is clearly already manifest in the three works of 1267. Each of the later is considered as a supplement or explanation of the earlier.

Yet despite the difficulties of untangling the authenticity and even identity of all the texts that are associated with Bacon, the purpose and nature of the three works of 1267 is fairly clear. A helpful starting point in this connection is the letter that Pope Clement IV sent to Bacon instructing him to send the works. I am afraid it requires more than usual attention on the part of listeners and readers. "We wish", the pope wrote, "that what you write should make clear to us what remedies it appears to you should be applied concerning the things that you recently indicated as the opening for such a great crisis, and this you should do as secretly as you can and without delay."[7] Now this is pretty cryptic, but it contains three key features: a great danger

---

[6] ad intelligentiam et perfectionem utriusque operis praecedentis, *Opus tertium* 1, ed. Brewer, p. 6.

[7] volumus...quatenus...per tuas nobis declares litteras quae tibi videntur adhibenda remedia circa illa quae nuper occasione tanti discriminis

is impending, Bacon has the key to dealing with it, and secrecy in this matter is essential. We shall return to all three points.

First, however, it is important to sketch out Bacon's picture of the physical universe, for, when it came to "the machine of this world", Roger Bacon had strong and distinctive views and these shaped much of his thinking in all areas. He believed that every point in the universe emitted radiation. Light was the most obvious example of such radiation and provided him with a recurrent model, but these emissions were not limited to light rays. Every point transmitted rays in all directions and also received them from every direction. This is what made it unique. As Bacon put it, regarding the earth, "all points on the earth are the centres of different horizons".[8] The patterns of rays emanating from or converging on a given point – patterns which Bacon terms pyramids, although we would perhaps say cones – are the most important determinants of the features of the universe. The most forceful rays are those that are the shortest and most direct. This, incidentally, is why "men devoting themselves to holiness" must try to avoid encountering short direct rays from delectable things, "such as women and foods and riches".[9]

---

intimastis et hoc quanto secretius poteris facias indilate: printed by Brewer, in *Fr. Rogeri Bacon opera* (as in note 4), p. 1 (the letter is dated June 1266).

[8] singula puncta terrae sunt centra diversorum horizontum: *Opus maius* 4, ed. Bridges 1, p. 397, tr. Burke, p. 272. His views are expressed most fully in *De multiplicatione specierum*, ed. David C. Lindberg in *Roger Bacon's Philosophy of Nature* (Oxford, 1983), pp. 1–269.

[9] primum et principale remedium quod in homine sit est ut in quinque sensus suos species rerum delectabilium, ut mulierum, et ciborum, et divitiarum... non recipiat secundum multiplicationem principalem... ideo homines sanctitati vacantes avertunt sensus ab omnibus rerum delectabilium speciebus quantum possunt... et praecipue cavent ne prope sint, ut vitent pyramides breviores, atque multiplicationes principales et rectas et ad angulos aequales: *Opus maius* 4, ed. Bridges 1, pp. 218–19, tr. Burke, p. 241.

Such a picture of the universe could be harnessed easily to astrology because, although these rays are not only astral, the rays emanating from the heavenly bodies will be uniquely determining forces. "All things vary," wrote Bacon, "because the vertexes of different pyramids containing the forces of the stars and of the parts of the heavens above the heads of the inhabitants come to the individual points of the earth".[10] "The first principle is that every point of the earth is the apex of a pyramid filled with the force of the heavens".[11] The influence of the heavens was indeed one of the main explanations for human variability. In his travels in northern France, Bacon noticed that the manners of the inhabitants differed from region to region, even on a local scale (he contrasts the Picards and the Normans, for example), and this is "due to the complexions of their bodies innate from the nature of the heavens".[12] Both manners and intellectual interests vary "according to the diversity of regions", for "the body is altered by the heavens and when the body is changed the mind is aroused".[13]

There might perhaps be a slight resonance of science fiction in this picture of a universe where every moment every spot is

[10] patet omnia variari . . . propter hoc quod coni diversarum pyramidum continentium virtutes stellarum et partium coeli super capita habitantium veniunt ad singula puncta terrae: *Opus maius* 4, ed. Bridges 1, p. 380, tr. Burke, p. 395.

[11] Primus vero articulus hic est, quod quilibet punctus terrae est conus unius pyramidis virtuosae coeli: *Opus maius* 4, ed. Bridges 1, p. 288 (with correction ibid. 3, p. 133), tr. Burke, p. 308.

[12] propter complexiones corporum innatas a natura coeli: *Opus maius* 4, ed. Bridges 1, p. 250, tr. Burke, p. 272.

[13] videmus in hominibus quod secundum diversitatem regionum habent mores diversos et occupant se in artibus et scientiis diversis: *Opus maius* 4, ed. Bridges 1, p. 301, tr. Burke, p. 320; per coelum alteratur corpus, et alterato corpore excitatur anima: *Opus maius* 4, ed. Bridges 1, p. 249, tr. Burke, p. 270.

bombarded with invisible rays, if it were not for the fact that modern theories of electromagnetic radiation are astonishingly similar.

Bacon had not invented this idea but was following in the footsteps, in a general way, of Robert Grosseteste, his older contemporary, and, more specifically, of the ninth-century Muslim scientist al-Kindi. Al-Kindi's treatise *On Rays* (*De radiis*) had been translated into Latin by the thirteenth century and had fairly wide circulation in England and northern France.[14] His most succinct statement on the subject in this work reads, "everything that has actual existence in the world of the elements sends out rays in every direction".[15] It is an intriguing point about intellectual history that what fascinated some people in ninth-century Baghdad could also fascinate some people in thirteenth-century Paris or Oxford. Four hundred years, two thousand miles, and a difference in religion did not necessarily make a theory irrelevant or repugnant. It is as if modern physicists drew their theories from sixteenth-century China.

Bacon was not the type of scholar to acknowledge his intellectual debts with much generosity. I am used to dealing with the conceit of past scholars (I say nothing of the present) because my doctoral thesis had as its subject Gerald of Wales, the Norman-Welsh ecclesiastic whose self-esteem led him to cite himself as

---

[14] Al-Kindi, "De Radiis", ed. M.-Th. D'Alverny and F. Hudry, *Archives d'histoire doctrinale et littéraire du moyen âge* 41 (1974), pp. 139–260; for the manuscript diffusion, p. 176. The Arabic original is lost, and it survives only in its Latin version. There is a brief but careful analysis in Claire Fanger, "Things Done Wisely by a Wise Enchanter: Negotiating the Power of Words in the Thirteenth Century", *Esoterica* 1 (1999), pp. 97–132, at pp. 101–5.

[15] omne quod actualem habet existentiam in mundo elementorum radios emittit in omnem partem: *De radiis* 3, ed. cit., p. 224.

"*quidam sapiens*", that is, "a certain wise man".[16] Bacon's arrogance is, however, of a different sort. Gerald's may perhaps have been laced with insecurity, with a need to prove himself. Bacon is, as far as one can judge, much more securely elitist. He thinks himself better than most people, although he is usually willing to concede that there might be a couple of scholars whom he might talk to. The characteristic Baconian position is as follows: not four Latins know Hebrew, Greek, and Arabic grammar; even Greeks and Jews don't know the grammar of their own languages properly; there are only two good mathematicians; only three scholars know the power of the science of optics.[17] As far as I can see, the happy few never number more than five, including Bacon himself. This is fairly austere, even in the embattled world of the scholarly egotist. It is significant that when Bacon defines the greatest Christian perfection as comprising virginity, voluntary poverty, and subjection to the will of another, he concludes "the greatest thing and the hardest is to subject oneself completely to the will of another, as everyone knows".[18]

A natural consequence of this view is that most people are excluded from the charmed circle. A key term of Bacon's elitism is hence *vulgus*, a word which can usually be translated as "the people, the great multitude, the public, mob, rabble, mass, crowd, throng". It would be a worthwhile scholarly task to chart its fortunes, uses, and general implications over the course of time. I cannot do that here but instead simply describe Bacon's use

---

[16] Gerald of Wales (Giraldus Cambrensis), *Speculum Duorum*, ed. Yves Lefèvre, R. B. C. Huygens, and Michael Richter (Cardiff, 1974), pp. 40, 102, 122, 180, with notes which give further references.

[17] *Opus tertium* 10–11, ed. Brewer, pp. 33–5, 37.

[18] virginitas...paupertas voluntaria...obligacio hominis ad voluntatem alterius, que tria sunt maxima perfectio.... set maximum quid et arduissimum est subicere se voluntati alterius omnino, ut quilibet novit: *Opus maius* 7. 4. 2. 8, ed. Massa, pp. 222–3, tr. Burke, p. 814.

of the word, for he employs it frequently but in a somewhat personal way. For him, the *vulgus* was not, usually, the great ignorant majority but something much more limited, namely, the average scholar or student – in contrast, of course, to himself. The *vulgus* could thus be a fairly small body. For instance, when discussing Aristotle's difficult concept of the "active intellect", a much debated topic in the thirteenth century, and considering whether it is part of the human soul, Bacon concludes "in no way does it follow that the active intellect is part of the soul, as the *vulgus* pretend".[19] It is extremely improbable that Bacon believed the populace as a whole had foolish opinions about the active intellect; the *vulgus* here must be, as in Robert Belle Burke's translation of the *Opus maius*, "the rank and file" of scholars, the ordinary ones – not like Bacon and his two or three peers.

Naturally, his theory of universal radiation ("multiplication of species" is Bacon's term for it) was, according to Bacon, not generally known. "Not one of the authorities," he writes, "neither of the old masters, nor of the moderns, has written about this; but I have laboured for ten years, as far as time permitted, and I have discoursed about everything as far as I was able."[20] Because of this general ignorance we are blind to what is actually the most important cause in our world. "These rays", writes Bacon, "produce every change in our world and in our bodies and souls, but because the emission of rays is not known to ordinary

[19] nullo modo sequitur quod intellectus agens sit pars animae, ut vulgus fingit: *Opus maius* 2. 5, ed. Bridges 3, p. 48, tr. Burke, p. 47. Aristotle's most important statement on the topic is *De anima* 3. 5. For a succinct description of Bacon's views on the active intellect, see Norman Kretzmann, Anthony Kenny, and Jan Pinborg (eds.), *The Cambridge History of Later Medieval Philosophy* (Cambridge, 1982), pp. 449–50.

[20] Nullus vero de auctoribus, nec de magistris antiquis, nec de modernis, scripsit de his; sed laboravi per annos decem, quantumcunque potui vacare, et discussi omnia ut potui: *Opus tertium* 11, ed. Brewer, p. 38.

scholars, except to three or four of the Latins, ... we do not perceive the wonderful actions of nature, which happen every day in us and in things before our eyes." Hence when we see something wonderful, we attribute it to the special working of God or to angels or demons or sheer chance. These things in fact have natural causes (*rationes naturales*).[21]

Bacon's commitment to a physical theory with such general explanatory power has, of course, made him a subject of interest to historians of science, and one thing they find especially intriguing is the emphasis he placed on what he calls *scientia experimentalis*. It is a phrase which could be – and has been – translated as "experimental science", although a case can also be made for translating it as "knowledge based on observation".[22] It is Bacon's stress on the importance of *experimentum* and *experientia* that has won him, for some, a heroic place

---

[21] Hae quidem species faciunt omnem mundi alterationem et corporum nostrorum et animarum. Sed quia haec multiplicatio specierum non est nota vulgo studentium, nec alicui nisi tribus vel quatuor Latinis, ... ideo mirabiles actiones naturae, quae tota die fiunt in nobis, et in rebus coram oculis nostris non percipimus; sed aestimamus eas fieri vel per specialem operationem divinam, vel per angelos, vel per daemones, vel a casu et fortuna.... omnis operatio creaturae est quodammodo a Deo. Sed hoc non excludit quin operationes fiant secundum rationes naturales: *Opus tertium* 26, ed. Brewer, pp. 99–100.

[22] Pierre Michaud-Quantin, *Etudes sur le vocabulaire philosophique de Moyen Age* (Rome, 1970), p. 220, suggests that *experientia* and *experimentum* should be translated "*observation*" rather than "*expérience*". For further discussion of the use of these terms in the thirteenth century, see Jacqueline Hamesse, "*Experientia/experimentum* dans les lexiques médiévaux et dans les textes philosophiques antérieurs au 14e siècle", in *Experientia: X Colloquio Internazionale del Lessico Intellettuale Europeo*, ed. M. Veneziani (Florence, 2002), pp. 77–90. See especially Jeremiah Hackett, "Roger Bacon on *Scientia Experimentalis*", in *Roger Bacon and the Sciences: Commemorative Essays*, ed. Jeremiah Hackett (Studien und Texte zur Geistesgeschichte des Mittelalters 57, Leiden, 1997), pp. 277–315.

in the history of science and explains why he has earned such resounding titles as "Crusader of Chemistry" or even "The First Scientist".[23]

There is no doubt of the importance of this *scientia experimentalis* in Bacon's scheme of things. The sixth section of the *Opus maius* is devoted to this subject and contains some stirring programmatic statements. "All things", writes Bacon, "must be verified by the path of experience."[24] Mere reasoning (*argumenta*) cannot bring us to certain truth. "He who wishes to rejoice without doubt in regard to the truths underlying phenomena must know how to devote himself to experiment".[25] A characteristic example is provided by the study of the rainbow, a topic naturally of great interest for Bacon, with his concern for rays and light. Mere reasoning will not yield solid conclusions about the nature of the rainbow, "but experiments on a large scale made with instruments ... are required". In an unusual moment of humility Bacon adds, "For this reason I do not think that in this matter I have grasped the whole truth, because I have not yet made all the experiments that are necessary"[26] – showing here a nice awareness that his results are provisional and subject to experimental verification.

[23] Leonard Jonathan Norton, *Crusaders of Chemistry: Six Makers of the Modern World* (Garden City, NY, 1930); Brian Clegg, *The First Scientist: A Life of Roger Bacon* (London, 2003).

[24] oportet ergo omnia certificari per viam experientiae: *Opus maius* 6. 1, ed. Bridges 2, p. 169, tr. Burke, p. 584; the text edited by Gasquet (as in note 4) reads "scientiam que nos ... certificaret per *veritatem* experientiae" (p. 510).

[25] Qui ergo vult sine demonstratione gaudere de veritatibus rerum, oportet quod experientiae sciat vacare: *Opus maius* 6. 1, ed. Bridges 2, p. 168, tr. Burke, p. 584.

[26] Unde argumenta non certificant haec, sed grandes experientiae per instrumenta perquiruntur ... Et propter hoc non reputo me attigisse hic plenam veritatem; quia nondum expertus sum omnia quae sunt hic necessaria: *Opus maius* 6. 12, ed. Bridges 2, p. 201, tr. Burke, p. 615.

Experimental science, in Bacon's view, is not simply pure science, dedicated to unravelling nature's mysteries, such as the properties of the rainbow. It is also strictly practical. This is where light is thrown on Pope Clement's cryptic remarks about the dangers threatening and Bacon's secret remedies for them. For in Bacon's view "experimental science", although, of course, "wholly unknown to the rank and file of students",[27] "teaches how wonderful instruments may be made, and uses them when made, and also considers all secret things owing to the advantages they may possess for the state and individuals".[28] This mention of "the state (*respublica*)" is significant, for experimental science includes applied science and hence has political importance.

Of the "wonderful instruments" that experimental science could produce, the most useful to the state were powerful weapons and, according to Bacon, the military application of science was already far advanced. Scientists, he wrote, "have discovered important arts against the foes of the state, so that without a sword or any weapon requiring physical contact they could destroy all who offer resistance".[29] Some of these inventions are not perceived by the senses, or are perceived only by smell; they include consuming, unquenchable fire; deafening sounds; and blinding flashes (Bacon gives a passing reference to children's fireworks at this point); elaborate poisons are also

---

[27] haec scientia experimentalis a vulgo studentium est penitus ignorata: *Opus maius* 6. 2, ed. Bridges 2, p. 172, tr. Burke, p. 587.

[28] haec [scientia] enim praecipit ut fiant instrumenta mirabilia, et factis utitur, et etiam cogitat omnia secreta propter utilitates reipublicae et personarum: *Opus maius* 6, ed. Bridges 2, p. 221, tr. Burke, p. 633.

[29] Et contra inimicos reipublicae adinvenerunt magnas artes, ut sine ferro, et absque eo quod tangerent aliquem, destruerent omnes resistentes: *Opus maius* 6, ed. Bridges 2, p. 217 (with correction ibid. 3, p. 143), tr. Burke, p. 629.

a possibility.[30] It was only the twentieth century that finally devised weapons capable of destroying a city in an instant, but the strong desire for them is ancient. In Bacon's urgent imagination, at least, there was already a fearful panoply of such armaments.

One area where Bacon's interest in optics and his concern with weapons of mass destruction intersected was mirrors. Mirrors can make a single object appear to be several: "therefore one man will appear many, and a single army will appear to be several ... to the advantage of the state images of this kind might profitably be produced."[31] Refraction could make a small army appear large; "we might cause the sun, moon and stars in appearance to descend here below, and similarly to appear above the heads of our enemies".[32] Mirrors could also be erected opposite enemy cities and armies to reveal what they were doing. "For in this way Julius Caesar, when he wished to subdue England, is said to have erected very large mirrors, in order that he might see in advance from the shores of Gaul the arrangement of the cities and camps of England".[33] This is a piece of information about

[30] *Opus maius* 6, ed. Bridges 2, pp. 217–18, tr. Burke, pp. 629–30.

[31] Et ideo unus homo videbitur plures, et unus exercitus plures ... et sic pro utilitatibus reipublicae ... possent hujusmodi apparitiones fieri utiliter: *Opus maius* 5. 3. 3. 3, ed. Bridges 2, p. 164, tr. Burke, pp. 580–1.

[32] sic etiam faceremus solem et lunam et stellas descendere secundum apparentiam hic inferius, et similiter super capita inimicorum apparere: *Opus maius* 5. 3. 3. 4, ed. Bridges 2, p. 166, tr. Burke, p. 582.

[33] Sic enim Julius Caesar, quando voluit Angliam expugnare, refertur maxima specula erexisse, ut a Gallicano littore dispositionem civitatum et castrorum Angliae praevideret: *Opus maius* 5. 3. 3. 3, ed. Bridges 2, p. 165, tr. Burke, pp. 580–1; the same story is in the *Epistola de secretis operibus artis naturae et de nullitate magiae*, ed. Brewer, *Fr. Rogeri Bacon opera* (as in note 4), pp. 523–51, at p. 534, although Bacon's authorship of this work is not universally acknowledged.

Caesar's British expedition that does not appear to be recorded elsewhere. [34]

One of the uses of such sophisticated military technology would be to fight the war against Islam. Bacon was strongly opposed to forcible conversion and wrote a powerful condemnation of the Teutonic Knights and their wars against the pagan Prussians,[35] but he clearly thought warfare between Christians and Muslims was a recurring feature of the scene and he promoted the idea that the "discoveries of science" could be used to destroy "enemies of the faith".[36] Mirror technology "might be used against unbelievers to inspire terror"[37] and if the Crusader states possessed a dozen giant mirrors, they would be able to repel the Muslims.[38] These were topical issues: while Bacon was writing the three works of 1267, the Egyptian Mamluks were making inroads into the crusader states, and in March of that year Louis IX of France (St Louis) took the Cross for the second time.

It was not only against the Muslims that the Christian West must be prepared, however. A far more ominous foe would soon be at hand. "All wise men believe," wrote Bacon, "that we are not far removed from the time of Antichrist".[39] From early in

[34] Homer Nearing, Jr., "The Legend of Julius Caesar's British Conquest", *Proceedings of the Modern Language Association of America* 64 (1949), pp. 889–929, at p. 911, notes Bacon's story but says he knows no source or parallel. It is repeated in *The Famous Historie* (as in note 1).

[35] *Opus maius* 7. 4. 2. 1, ed. Massa, p. 200, tr. Burke, pp. 796–7.

[36] inimicos fidei, destruendos magis per opera sapientiae, quam per arma: *Opus maius* 6, ed. Bridges 2, p. 221, tr. Burke, p. 633.

[37] contra infideles possent hujusmodi apparitiones fieri utiliter et in terrorem: *Opus maius* 5. 3. 3. 3, ed. Bridges 2, p. 164, tr. Burke, 581.

[38] *Opus tertium* 36, ed. Brewer, p. 116.

[39] Et creditur ab omnibus sapientibus quod non sumus multum remoti a temporibus Antichristi: *Opus maius* 4, ed. Bridges 1, p. 402, tr. Burke, pp. 416–17.

13. ANTICHRIST From its origins, Christianity had taught that the world would come to an end in dramatic catastrophe, culminating in the Last Judgment and a new heaven and a new earth. Some people, in some times and places, thought this might be happening soon. One of the events characterizing the End would be the rise of Antichrist, a great deceiver and persecutor. Needless to say, over the course of time many figures were

its history, one might say from its inception, Christianity has been a religion of the Last Things, and its Scripture not only begins at the beginning but ends at the end. The Book of Revelation describes the last curtain call of the present world and is a continual invitation to systematize the confusion of the present by giving it apocalyptic significance. The urge to do so is understandable. It is hard to bear if some tyrant under whom we suffer is just a cruel, passing, and meaningless monster. If, however, he is a horn of the beast of the apocalypse, then we know we are playing our part in the grand drama of the end of time.

Bacon lived in a richly apocalyptic age. The Holy Roman Emperor Frederick II, frequently and luridly identified with the Antichrist, died in 1250, and in the thirteenth century, the most commonly predicted date for the coming of the End was the year 1260, just seven years before Bacon produced his trio of works (at least it was the most commonly predicted date until 1261). It was Bacon's own order, the Franciscans, that was most deeply affected by radical apocalypticism, the strand known as Joachism from the name of its inspirer, Joachim of Fiore.[40]

Obtaining a precise date for the arrival of Antichrist would obviously be useful and Bacon thought that this "time of Antichrist" might perhaps be predicted both through astronomy

---

[40] The classic study in English is Marjorie Reeves, *The Influence of Prophecy in the Later Middle Ages: A Study in Joachimism* (Oxford, 1969).

---

13 (*continued*) identified as Antichrist. In Roger Bacon's lifetime, one of the most common identifications was with the Emperor Frederick II. After his death in 1250, many friars, including Bacon, still expected the End soon: "All wise men believe," wrote Bacon, "that we are not far removed from the time of Antichrist". Scientific research was one way to prepare. (Bodleian Library, University of Oxford, MS. Auct. D. 4. 17, fol. 7r (Apocalypse); English, mid-thirteenth century.)

and through a thorough search of the ancient prophecies of Sibyl, Merlin, and the rest, as well as the more recent ones of Joachim.[41] Contrary to the opinions of some, he considered that the Mongol invasions of Genghis Khan and his successors were, in themselves, "not sufficient to fix the time of Antichrist",[42] but it might well be that the Mongols would destroy Islam, and it was certain that Antichrist would come only after the destruction of Islam.

The date of this event, the fall of Islam, could be established by reference to Muslim authors themselves, for, surprising though it may seem, it is actually the case that the Islamic astrologers of the ninth century had already employed the techniques of historical astrology to calculate how long Islam would endure. Abu Mashar, known as Albumazar in the medieval West, the great Muslim philosopher of the ninth century, in his work *The Great Conjunctions*, which was available to the Latin West since its translation into Latin in the twelfth century, gave an exact prediction: Islam could not last more than 693 years.[43] These were, of course, Islamic years, slightly shorter than Christian years, and Bacon was well aware of this. "It is now the 665th year of the Arabs," he wrote, which corresponds exactly to the time he was writing, that is, A.D.1267. The fall of Islam must

---

[41] *Opus maius* 4, ed. Bridges 1, p. 269, tr. Burke, p. 290; cf. his letter to the pope, ed. Gasquet (as in n. 4), pp. 514–15.

[42] discursus Tartarorum non sufficit certificare tempus de adventu Antichristi: *Opus maius* 7. 1. 3, ed. Massa, p. 17, tr. Burke, p. 645.

[43] Albumasar (Abu Ma'shar), *De magnis coniunctionibus* 2. 8. 5, ed. Keiji Yamamoto and Charles Burnett, *On Historical Astrology: The Book of Religions and Dynasties (On the Great Conjunctions)* (2 vols., Leiden, 2000), 1, p. 127 (English translation of the Arabic), 2, p. 83 (Latin). See 2, pp. xiii–xv, for discussion of the date, place, and authorship of the Latin translation. Al-Kindi's letter expressing the same view is also edited there, with the relevant passage at 1, p. 533.

thus take place by 693 in the Muslim calendar, that is, 1294 on the Christian calendar.[44] As we know, Islam did not disappear in 1294, but it is poignant that this year is one frequently given as the date of Bacon's own death.

Bacon thus considered that the destruction of Islam would take place within twenty-seven years of the time he was writing, and he thought it possible that Antichrist would come soon after.[45] This was the "great crisis" that Pope Clement had referred to in his letter to Bacon, a crisis for which Bacon had the remedies. "I am writing", says Bacon, "on account of the dangers that are befalling and will befall the Christians through Antichrist".[46] Threat and remedy were closely related, for one needed Antichrist's own weapons to counter him, and Antichrist himself was a scientist, able to employ "the potency of science".[47] Bacon's long section in the *Opus maius* on experimental science concludes with the reflection that "Antichrist will use the discoveries of science to crush and confound the power of this world".[48] As one might have anticipated, Antichrist will use powerful concave mirrors to burn up cities and

---

[44] *Opus maius* 4, ed. Bridges 1, p. 266, tr. Burke, p. 287; et Albumazar in primo libro Coniunctionum docet quod ad plus non durabit secta illa nisi per 693 annos; et iam transiverunt 665: *Opus maius* 7. 4. 2. 6, ed. Massa, p. 215, with reference to Albumasar, *De magnis coniunctionibus* 2. 7 (using the 1489 Augsburg printing), tr. Burke, p. 808. The Muslim year 665 corresponds to October 1266–September 1267 and the Muslim year 693 to December 1293–November 1294. Thanks to Hugh Kennedy for providing these equivalences.

[45] *Opus maius* 4, ed. Bridges 1, p. 268, tr. Burke, pp. 288–90.

[46] scribo . . . propter pericula quae continguunt et contingent Christianis . . . per Antichristum: *Opus maius* 4, ed. Bridges 1, p. 399, tr. Burke, p. 415.

[47] ipse utetur potestate sapientiae: *Opus maius* 4, ed. Bridges 1, p. 399, tr. Burke, p. 415.

[48] opera sapientiae . . . quibus Antichristus copiose et efficaciter utetur, ut omnem hujus mundi potentiam conterat et confundat: *Opus maius* 6, ed. Bridges 2, p. 221, tr. Burke, p. 633.

armies.[49] As always, weapons of mass destruction were double-edged.

What were the remedies? As usual, a little cash would help. Bacon claimed that in the long years during which he had laboured at the study of wisdom, characteristically "disregarding the crowd's approach" (*neglecto sensu vulgi*), he had spent at least £2000 on these matters.[50] It has been assumed that this was before he became a Franciscan.[51] However, Bacon explains his delay in replying to the pope's request for the works of 1267, when he was certainly a Franciscan, partly from his lack of money, which was necessary for copyists and so on actually to produce the manuscript books. He had sent a plea for funds to his family back in England, he says, but they had been financially ruined by the Montfortians, the rebel barons, and he had not even received a reply.[52] Even a friar had his research expenses.

The solution to such problems was, according to Bacon, state funding for science. He repeatedly highlights the need for princes to back scientific inquiry with concrete practical help. Exploration of the equatorial regions, for instance, had been impeded naturally by the distance but even more by "the negligence of princes who should have aided philosophers in this matter".[53] The determination of accurate latitude and longitude requires "apostolic

---

[49] *Opus maius* 4. 2. 2, ed. Bridges 1, p. 116, tr. Burke, p. 135.

[50] Nam per viginti annos quibus specialiter laboravi in studio sapientiae, neglecto sensu vulgi, plus quam duo millia librarum ego posui in his: *Opus tertium* 17, ed. Brewer, p. 59.

[51] For example, "Since entry into the Order would require a vow of poverty, it seems that Bacon must have spent his two thousand pounds while still a secular", *Roger Bacon's Philosophy of Nature*, ed. David C. Lindberg (Oxford, 1983), p. xx.

[52] *Opus tertium* 3, ed. Brewer, p. 16.

[53] propter negligentiam principum qui philosophos deberent juvare in hac parte: *Opus maius* 4, ed. Bridges 1, p. 296, tr. Burke, p. 316.

or imperial authority" or "the aid of some great king who will furnish the means to men of science"[54] ("some great king" in this period is often light code for the king of France, St Louis at this time). It is worth noting, in this context of geographical exploration, that Bacon's view of the world was a wide one. He was familiar with William of Rubruck, the Franciscan traveller mentioned in the previous chapter, whose journey to Asia had given him a taste for fermented mare's milk as well as made him sceptical about dog-heads. Bacon had not only read William of Rubruck's account of his journeys among the Mongols but has also "conferred with its author".[55] Such links with the wide Franciscan world provided Bacon with unusual knowledge. It is the reason he can disagree with the ancient authors who thought that the Caspian Sea was an arm of the Ocean[56] and expound a view of world religions that included not only the traditional "religions of the book", Judaism, Christianity, and Islam, but also Buddhism.[57]

[54] nisi per apostolicam auctoritatem vel imperialem, aut per auxilium alicujus regis magni praebentis philosophantibus adjutorium: *Opus maius* 4, ed. Bridges 1, p. 300, tr. Burke, p. 320.

[55] quem librum diligenter vidi, et cum ejus auctore contuli: *Opus maius* 4, ed. Bridges 1, p. 305, tr. Burke, p. 324; Bacon also mentions the book of John of Piano Carpini, who undertook a journey to the Mongols in 1245–7: *Opus maius* 4, ed. Bridges 1, p. 371, tr. Burke, p. 386; *Opus maius* 7. 4. 1. 1, ed. Massa, p. 190, tr. Burke, p. 789.

[56] *Opus maius* 4, ed. Bridges 1, p. 354, tr. Burke, p. 372. Bacon explains the error of such ancient authorities as Isidore and Pliny from the fact that they did not have "experientiam certam" but wrote "ex rumore"; he, on the other hand, has been able to gather information "in libris de moribus Tartarorum". It has been pointed out that "The first medieval European to describe [the Caspian] as landlocked may have been William of Rubruck": Scott D. Westrem (ed.), *The Hereford Map: A Transcription and Translation of the Legends with Commentary* (Terrarum Orbis 1, Turnhout, 2001), p. 70 n. 145.

[57] On Bacon's theory of religion, see Erich Heck, *Roger Bacon: Ein mittelalterlicher Versuch einer historischen und systematischen*

In Bacon's opinion, the perfect relationship between ruler and philosopher was that of Aristotle and Alexander. He tells how Aristotle, on Alexander's authority, sent out 2,000 men "to gain experimental knowledge of all things that are on the face of the earth";[58] and this relationship of philosopher and king was of mutual benefit, for while Alexander funded Aristotle's researches, then "by the paths of knowledge Aristotle was able to hand over the world to Alexander".[59] For "Alexander did not subdue the world by the force of arms but, with the advice of Aristotle, with the works of science".[60]

State support would help prepare the Latins for the coming threat: "it would be easy to meet the future perils in the time of Antichrist if prelates and princes promoted study and investigated the secrets of nature and art".[61] He gives a concrete example from his own time of how scientific research might help the Christian commonwealth. In July 1264, a comet had appeared, and, as subsequently became clear, it had portended wars in England, Spain, Italy, and elsewhere. Bacon reflects, "Oh how great

Religionswissenschaft (Bonn, 1957); Amanda Louise Power, "The Views of Roger Bacon on Geography, World Religions and the Defence of Christendom as Expressed in His *Opus maius*" (unpublished Ph.D., Cambridge University, 2003), esp. pp. 139–61. His knowledge of the relations of the pagan Prussians and the Teutonic Knights (see note 35) also came via Dominicans and Franciscans in Germany and Poland.

[58] Aristoteles auctoritate Alexandri misit duo millia hominum per diversa loca mundi ut experientur omnia quae sunt in superficie terrae: *Opus maius* 6. 1, ed. Bridges 2, p. 169, tr. Burke, p. 585.

[59] per vias sapientiae potuit Aristoteles mundum tradere Alexandro: *Opus maius* 6, ed. Bridges 2, p. 222, tr. Burke, p. 634.

[60] Alexander, de consilio Aristotelis, mundum non armorum potentia, sed operibus sapientiae prostravit: *Opus tertium* 36, ed. Brewer, p. 117.

[61] futura pericula in temporibus Antichristi, quibus cum Dei gratia facile esset obviare, si praelati et principes studium promoverent et secreta naturae et artis indagarent: *Opus maius* 6, ed. Bridges 2, p. 222, tr. Burke, p. 634.

14. ARISTOTLE TEACHING ALEXANDER. For the Middle Ages, Aristotle was "the Philosopher" and Alexander the greatest conqueror. Aristotle was in fact Alexander's tutor, and this medieval illustration offers an imaginative depiction of the great philosopher teaching the great conqueror. For Roger Bacon, the relationship between Aristotle and Alexander provided a model of how learning could support political and military power and how the state could, in return, support scientific research. "Alexander", wrote Bacon, "did not subdue the world by the force of arms but, with the advice of Aristotle, with the works of science." (The Pierpont Morgan Library, New York. MS M.771, fol. 103. Fiore di vertu. [ca.1460].)

an advantage might have been secured to the Church of God if the characteristics of the heavens in those times had been discerned beforehand by scientists and understood by prelates and princes and transferred to a zeal for peace".[62]

Apart from the proper funding of science, the West needed to take seriously the issue of language training. Bacon's thinking is in general characterized by a strong awareness of language as central and defining.[63] He repeatedly stressed the necessity of learning foreign languages; he was extremely sensitive to the problems of translating from one language into another; and his most common label of group self-identification was not "English" or "Christian", let alone "European", but "Latin", a term which indicates much more than a linguistic identity, of course, but certainly includes and emphasizes it. Again and again Bacon signals this important self-perception. He can even talk of the "commonwealth, state or republic of the Latins (*respublica Latinorum*)".[64]

Of course this identity, as a Latin, implies an upbringing as a *litteratus*, a member of the tiny international elite trained in this language, but, in Bacon's usage, it is far from being triumphalist or self-congratulatory, as self-designations usually tend to be.

---

[62] O quanta utilitas ecclesiae Dei potuisset procurari, si coeli qualitas istorum temporum fuisset praevisa a sapientibus, et praelatis et principibus cognita, et pacis studio mancipata: *Opus maius* 4, ed. Bridges 1, p. 386, tr. Burke, pp. 400–1; the comet of 1264 provoked wide comment in many different parts of Europe: Radivoj Radic, "George Pachymeres and Roger Bacon on the Comet from 1264", in *Srednovekovna khristiianska Evropa: iztok i zapad/Medieval Christian Europe: East and West*, ed. Vasil Gyuzelev and Anisava Miltenova (Sofia, 2002), pp. 485–9.

[63] See David Luscombe, "Roger Bacon and Language", in *Britannia latina: Latin in the Culture of Great Britain from the Middle Ages to the Twentieth Century*, ed. Charles Burnett and Nicholas Mann (Warburg Institute Colloquia 8, 2005), pp. 42–54.

[64] For example, *Opus maius* 3. 12, ed. Bridges 3, p. 119, tr. Burke, p. 109.

The Latins are in fact debtors in the world of culture. Neglect of languages (as of mathematics), he writes, has undermined "the learning of the Latins (*studium Latinorum*)";[65] "not one Latin (*nullus Latinus*)" will understand scripture or philosophy without such linguistic knowledge.[66]

Bacon had a strong awareness of where he stood in history. Given his interests, it is no surprise that the history he located himself in was the history of philosophy and, more specifically, the history of the transmission of philosophical knowledge. His view was a long one. God first revealed philosophy to the biblical patriarchs and prophets; this was renewed by Aristotle— and Bacon had begun his scholarly life by lecturing on Aristotle[67] – and continued by the great Muslim scholars such as Avicenna and Averroes. Hence it was essential for the Latins to master Hebrew, Greek, and Arabic.[68] On the subject of astronomical prediction, for example, "the Latins have nothing of value except from other tongues".[69] Bacon looked back on the Latin authors of the early Middle Ages and even those of the so-called twelfth-century Renaissance, such as Hugh of St. Victor, as deeply handicapped by their ignorance of the writings of the Greeks and the Arabs.[70] Bacon considered that in the early

---

[65] *Opus maius* 1. 12, ed. Bridges 3, p. 26, tr. Burke, p. 27; *Opus maius* 4. 1. 1, ed. Bridges 1, p. 97, tr. Burke, p. 116.

[66] *Opus maius* 3. 1, ed. Bridges 3, p. 81, tr. Burke, p. 76.

[67] His Aristotelian commentaries are published in *Opera hactenus inedita Rogeri Baconis*, ed. Robert Steele and Ferdinand M. Delorme (16 vols., Oxford, 1905–40), vols. 7–8, 10–13.

[68] Latini nihil magnificum scire possunt sine notitia harum linguarum: *Opus tertium* 10, ed. Brewer, p. 32; this is the theme of Part Three of the *Opus maius*.

[69] Latini nihil quid valet habent nisi ab aliis linguis: *Opus maius* 4, ed. Bridges 1, p. 389, tr. Burke, p. 405.

[70] See especially *Opus maius* 1. 13–15, ed Bridges 3, pp. 28–33, tr. Burke, pp. 29–34.

Middle Ages, the Latins employed scientific knowledge in limited spheres. They studied only astronomy, because it was important for determining the calendar, and music for church services. It was only during his own lifetime that the situation had begun to change, and even now the absorption of this new knowledge was certainly not complete. He was aware of the relative recentness of acceptance of Aristotle, Avicenna, and Averroes in translation.[71]

Such awareness of the "poverty of the Latins" in cultural matters can be found among some thinkers as early as the eleventh century,[72] but it is especially central to Bacon's outlook. I do not know when it became common to call the infusion of Greco-Arabic material into the Latin West during the twelfth and thirteenth centuries "the translation movement", but, whenever it was, Bacon would have approved of the label.[73] He tried to make a contribution himself, producing grammars of Greek and Hebrew, proposing the production of a dictionary of loan words in Latin,[74] and, in his *Compendium studii philosophiae* of the early 1270s, listing words of Greek derivation in common use in

---

[71] *Opus maius* 1. 9, ed. Bridges 3, p. 21, tr. Burke, p. 22. See in general Richard Lemay, "Roger Bacon's Attitude toward the Latin Translations and Translators of the Twelfth and Thirteenth Centuries", in *Roger Bacon and the Sciences*, ed. Hackett (as in note 4), pp. 25–47.

[72] For example, Alfanus' translation of Nemesius refers to "Latinorum... penuria": cited by Marie-Thérèse d'Alverny, "Translations and Translators", in *Renaissance and Renewal in the Twelfth Century*, ed. Robert Benson and Giles Constable (Cambridge, MA, and Oxford, 1982), pp. 421–62, at p. 426. She refers to this as "a topical formula of many translators".

[73] It is a phrase also applied to the period of translation from Greek and Syriac into Arabic in the eighth, ninth, and tenth centuries of the Christian era. See, for example, Dimitri Gutas, *Greek Thought, Arabic Culture: The Graeco-Arabic Translation Movement in Baghdad and Early 'Abbasid Society* (London, 1998).

[74] *Opus maius* 3. 6, ed. Bridges 3, p. 107, tr. Burke, p. 98.

Latin, from *abyssus* to *zona*, as well as specialized ecclesiastical and scholarly terms.[75]

Knowledge of languages was, of course, necessary not only for philosophy but also for the practical purposes of trade, diplomacy, and mission. It would be especially useful, Bacon thought, in the colonial areas of the Mediterranean where Latins ruled over Greeks, Syrians, Arabs, and others, whereas trade was vital to the Latins because "medicines and all precious things (*medicinalia et omnia pretiosa*)" are imported.[76] He was outraged that no one could be found in the University of Paris or indeed the whole of France who could translate a letter sent from the Sultan of Egypt to St Louis (the West has obviously been searching for Arabic language expertise for a long time).[77]

THE CORRESPONDENCE BETWEEN BACON AND POPE CLEMENT specified that secrecy be observed and secrecy and secret knowledge was an obsession of Bacon's. Life can be prolonged, he wrote, and the effects of old age retarded, "but these matters have always been hidden from the rank and file of philosophers".[78] One of the reasons for emphasizing the study of foreign languages was on account of the "great secrets of all the branches

---

[75] *Compendium studii philosophiae* 6, ed. Brewer in *Fr. Rogeri Bacon opera* (as in note 4), pp. 393–519, at pp. 441–4; for the date, see ibid. 3, p. 414, where Bacon refers to "the lord Clement, predecessor of the present pope (*domini Clementis, praedecessori istius papae*)"; this must therefore have been written during the pontificate of Gregory X (1271–6).

[76] *Opus maius* 3. 11, ed. Bridges 3, p. 118, tr. Burke, p. 108; 3. 12, ed. Bridges 3, p. 119, tr. Burke, p. 109.

[77] *Opus maius* 3. 12, ed. Bridges 3, p. 120, tr. Burke, p. 110.

[78] Sed haec et hujusmodi secretorum secretissima semper fuerunt occultata a vulgo philosophantium: *Opus maius* 6, ed. Bridges 2, p. 209, tr. Burke, pp. 621.

of knowledge (*scientiarum et artium*) and the hidden things of nature that have not yet been translated".[79] It is entirely appropriate that Bacon should have produced his own edition of the Pseudo-Aristotelian *Secretum secretorum* (the "Secret of Secrets"), complete with introduction and glosses.[80] In that work, Aristotle had supposedly promised Alexander "the greatest secret of secrets" and urged him to keep the mystery to himself.[81]

Did Bacon have any reasonable grounds for being secretive? I mentioned at the start of this chapter the disagreement among scholars about Bacon's imprisonment by his own order. The evidence for this is explicit, but for some a little late to be trusted, coming as it does from a Franciscan chronicle of the fourteenth century. Here we read that the minister-general of the order "condemned and reproved the teaching of Friar Roger Bacon the Englishman ... which contained some suspect novelties" and that Roger himself was imprisoned. The same source adds that the pope was also induced to condemn "that dangerous teaching". From the names of the minister-general and pope involved, this must have taken place around 1278, a decade or so after Bacon had produced his great work.[82]

---

[79] magna secreta scientiarum et artium et naturae arcana quae nondum sunt translata: *Opus maius* 3. 2, ed. Bridges 3, p. 85, tr. Burke, p. 79.

[80] *Secretum secretorum*, ed. Robert Steele (Opera hactenus inedita Rogeri Baconi 5, Oxford, 1920).

[81] Inprimis, O Alexander, tradere tibi volo secretorum maximum secretum, et divina potencia juvet te ad perficiendum propositum, et ad celandum archanum: ibid. 3. 1, p. 114; cf. Aristotle's statement to Alexander promising "the greatest secret" which would provide "an advantage for the state and for every one his desire": Aristoteles dixit ad Alexandrum 'volo ostendere secretum maximum' ... procuraret bonum reipublicae et omnibus desideratum: *Opus maius* 6, ed. Bridges 2, p. 215, tr. Burke, p. 627.

[82] Hic Generalis frater Hieronymus de multorum fratrum consilio condemnavit et reprobavit doctrinam fratris Rogerii Bachonis Anglici, sacrae

This was not the only crack of the ecclesiastical whip at this time. In the spring of 1277, the bishop of Paris condemned a total of 219 erroneous beliefs which had been circulating among the students and teachers of Paris. These beliefs are of an enormously miscellaneous type, but it is clear that one of the general targets of the condemnations was naturalism, the idea that the physical universe was governed by its own natural laws and could best be explained in those terms. To take one example, I turn to condemnation number 90, concerning the eternity of the universe. There was vigorous debate on this subject in the thirteenth century, for whereas the Bible begins with creation from nothing and ends with the end of the world, Aristotle and some of his Arabic followers suggested that the physical universe has neither beginning nor end. Here is the relevant article, which describes the erroneous belief:

> The natural philosopher must plainly deny that the universe was created from nothing, because he relies on natural causes and natural reasons. The believer, however, can deny that the universe is eternal, because he relies on supernatural causes.[83]

theologiae magistri, continentem aliquas novitates suspectas, propter quas fuit idem Rogerius carceri condemnatus, praecipiendo omnibus fratribus, ut nullus illam teneret, sed ipsam vitaret ut per Ordinem reprobatam. Super hoc etiam scripsit domino Papae Nicolao praefato, ut per eius auctoritatem doctrina illa periculosa totaliter sopiretur: *Chronica XXIV Generalium Ordinis Minorum, Analecta Franciscana* 3 (1897), p. 360. "Hieronymus" is Jerome of Ascoli, who was minister-general from May 1274 to May 1279; the pope is Nicholas III, elected November 1277. The chronicle extends to 1374, but much of it was probably compiled prior to 1369: ibid., pp. VIII–IX.

[83] Quod naturalis philosophus debet negare simpliciter mundi novitatem, quia innititur causis naturalibus, et rationibus naturalibus. Fidelis autem potest negare mundi eternitatem, quia innititur causis supernaturalibus: *Chartularium Universitatis Parisiensis* 1 (1200–1286), ed. Henri Denifle (Paris, 1889), no. 473, p. 548. There is a new edition, with discussion, in David Piché and Claude Lafleur, *La Condemnation parisienne de 1277* (Paris, 1999).

It is worth stressing that this article does not constitute a simple assertion of creationism. It is more specific than that. It insists that it is not acceptable to posit a realm of natural causes and a realm of supernatural causes (and we do have here a relatively early use of that term). The bishop of Paris did not accept that there could be a truce between two incompatible truths, the philosopher's and the theologian's. Natural philosophy cannot claim its own sphere and its own rules.

The close coincidence in time between the supposed condemnation of Bacon's dangerous novelties and the Parisian list of 219 errors makes one wonder if there is any connection. Bacon's belief in astrology, for instance, could certainly have seemed suspicious, and astrological determinism is one of the doctrines condemned in 1277.[84] To take one instance, Bacon held the view that the pattern of the heavens at the time of Christ's conception was not only a *sign* of the Incarnation but also had a natural and substantial effect that co-operated with and aided the Virgin Mary. Even though he insisted that this influence operated only as far as "natural things" were concerned, [85] his approach might nevertheless seem perilously close to subjecting the salvation story to the governing power of the heavens.[86]

Moreover, and here I turn to my final subject in this brief overview of the complex thought of Roger Bacon, some people might worry about the place of magic in his thinking.

One of the great classic works on medieval science, by the American historian Lynn Thorndike, the first volumes of which

[84] For example, clauses 206–7, ibid., p. 555.

[85] consideratis pure naturalibus: *Opus maius* 4, ed. Bridges 1, p. 268, tr. Burke, p. 289.

[86] Paul L. Sidelko, "The Condemnation of Roger Bacon", *Journal of Medieval History* 22 (1996), pp. 69–81; Power, "The Views of Roger Bacon" (as in note 57), pp. 54–9, is sceptical.

were published in 1923, bears the significant title *The History of Magic and Experimental Science*. "My idea", he wrote, "is that magic and experimental science have been connected in their development...and that the history of both...can be better understood by studying them together."[87] This learned scholar did not see any way to deal with medieval science without dealing with magic. This is particularly true when studying Roger Bacon.

Bacon's express position on magic is remarkable. He describes the value and importance of a whole range of activities that, we feel, almost anyone would label "magic", and then insists that, whatever else they are, they are not magic.

Take the example of *"fascinatio"*, a word cognate of course with modern English "fascination", but best translated as "hostile enchantment". *Fascinatio* springs from a strong "desire to do harm"[88] and the most familiar form of it is the so-called evil eye, although there were many other variants. Bacon himself had witnessed a particularly striking manifestation of the power of fascination, for he had personally observed the Shepherds' Crusade of 1251, when thousands of herdsmen and other poor workers assembled under a charismatic preacher with the intention of marching off to fight Islam and save Christianity. As might have been expected, the movement ended in chaos and disaster, and Bacon's opinion was that it had actually been inspired by the enemies of Christendom. The leader of the Shepherds' Crusade, as in the case of the somewhat similar Children's

---

[87] Thorndike, *History of Magic* (as in note 2) 1, p. 2. Thorndike acknowledged the influence of Frazer on this perspective: "Frazer has, of course, repeatedly made the point that modern science is an outgrowth from primitive magic", ibid., p. 5 n. 1. Thorndike subsequently covered the period up to and including the seventeenth century in six further volumes.

[88] desiderium nocendi...ad hoc reducitur fascinatio...: *Opus maius* 4. 4. 7, ed. Bridges 1, p. 143, tr. Burke, p. 164.

Crusade of 1212, had in fact been sent by the Mongols or the Muslims "and they had some means by which they fascinated the people".[89] Bacon had noticed that the leader of the Shepherds carried some special object in his hand, which was obviously the transmitter for this mesmerizing power. Bacon believed that fascination, in what he calls its "true meaning", was efficacious: "If some malign soul should think strongly on infecting someone else, and should ardently desire it, and definitely design it, and earnestly consider that he is able to harm, there is no doubt that nature will obey the thoughts of his mind...". He then adds, with emphasis, "and still this is not magic".[90]

It is as if he were describing an animal and said, "It is very large, has thick grey skin, a long trunk and tusks. There are two varieties, one in Africa, one in India. But it is *not* an elephant, no, certainly not an elephant." Bacon's febrile insistence naturally arouses the suspicion that he doth protest too much. As Claire Fanger has put it, "Bacon's largely negative use of the term 'magic' seems to be part of a systematically employed rhetorical strategy designed principally...to put his own activities above suspicion precisely *because* he was conscious that they had a magical dimension".[91]

Bacon certainly was sensitive to the dangers of accusations of magic. He himself believed that images carved in the right way, when the pattern of the heavens was appropriate, could have enormous power. "If one happens at chosen times to carve

---

[89] habuerunt aliqua opera unde fascinabant plebem: *Opus maius* 4, ed. Bridges 1, pp. 401, tr. Burke, p. 417.

[90] si ulterius aliqua anima maligna cogitet fortiter de infectione alterius, atque ardenter desideret et certitudinaliter intendat, atque vehementer consideret se posse nocere, non est dubium quin natura obediet cogitationibus animae...et adhuc non est magicum: *Opus maius* 4, ed. Bridges 1, p. 398, tr. Burke, p. 414.

[91] Fanger, "Things Done Wisely" (as in note 14), p. 113.

images after the face of the heavens," he writes, "all harmful things can be repelled and useful things promoted".[92] But, he says, those who carve astronomical images do not venture "to speak about these works in public. For they are straightaway called magicians".[93] Bacon's position on the inherent power of words made him even more vulnerable.[94] Under the proper scientific conditions, he thought that great effects could be achieved by utterances alone. There is "nothing magical or foolish"[95] in believing in the efficacy of the word spoken when the circumstances are right. If words are uttered with deep thought and great desire and right intention and firm confidence, they have great power.[96] "An unspotted soul, strong desire and clear intention" on the part of the speaker could combine with "the power of the heavens" to produce remarkable effects.[97] He is not afraid to use even such a suspect term as *carmina* – "incantations". Incantations are "words uttered in accordance with the intention of the rational soul, which receive in the mere act of pronouncing them the force of the heavens...the matter of the world is changed to many wonderful forms if those means are

[92] si contingit temporibus electis eas [sc. imagines] sculpere ad vultus coelorum, omnia nociva repelli possunt et utilia promoveri: *Opus maius* 4, ed. Bridges 1, p. 394, tr. Burke, p. 409; for the debate on such images see Nicholas Weill-Parot, *Les Images astrologiques au Moyen Age et à la Renaissance* (Paris, 2002).

[93] vix est aliquis ausus loqui de his operibus in publico. Statim enim vocantur magici: *Opus maius* 4, ed. Bridges 1, p. 394, tr. Burke, p. 410.

[94] See Irène Rosier, *La Parole comme acte: sur la grammaire et la sémantique au XIIIe siècle* (Paris, 1994), esp. chapter 6.

[95] nihil est magicum vel insanum: *Opus maius* 4, ed. Bridges 1, p. 399, tr. Burke, p. 415.

[96] *Opus tertium* 26, ed. Brewer, pp. 95–100, gives a succinct summary of this view.

[97] anima immaculata et desiderio forti et certa intentione et virtute caelesti: *Opus maius* 3. 14, ed. Bridges 3, p. 125, tr. Burke, p. 115.

correctly employed".[98] The power of incantations was an aspect of his theory of universal radiation, for the utterances themselves generated rays. Bacon could find this opinion too in al-Kindi's book on rays, for by far the longest chapter in that work is titled "The Power of Words (*De virtute verborum*)"[99] and it starts from the simple premise, "utterances produce rays".[100] So the effects of utterances, being part of the general theory of universal radiation, also belonged to the world of natural causation.

Magic had got a bad press by mixing in the wrong company. It was the "accursed magicians" and "old women" who had brought such techniques into disrepute by their indiscriminate and unscientific methods and claims.[101] It was partly a matter of classification. After mentioning the powerful multiplication of species that can take place when an utterance is made under the right conditions, especially the disposition of the stars, Bacon says, "If this is called fascination, we can change the name if we wish"; it is only "magicians and accursed old women" who believe that fascination can operate indiscriminately.[102] Nor it is the mere technique that is at issue, for the same thing can be used for different ends: "with a knife I can cut bread or wound a man. So likewise through words a wise man can work wisely and a magician magically. The former acts through a natural power,

---

[98] carmina sunt verba ex intentione animae rationalis prolata, virtutem coeli in ipsa pronunicatione recipientia...Alteratur enim mundi materia ad multas passiones mirabiles, si recte fierent ista...: *Opus maius* 4, ed. Bridges 1, p. 395, tr. Burke, p. 411.

[99] Al-Kindi, *De radiis* (as in note 14) 6, pp. 233–50.

[100] voces in actum producte radios faciunt: ibid., p. 233.

[101] magici maledicti...vetulae; vetulae sortilegae et magici: *Opus maius* 4, ed. Bridges 1, pp. 395, 398, tr. Burke, pp. 411, 413.

[102] Et si hoc vocetur fascinatio, nomen, si volumus, possumus mutare... magici et vetulae maledictae non considerant fascinationem per has vias: *Opus maius* 4, ed. Bridges 1, p. 399, tr. Burke, p. 415.

the latter either achieves nothing or the devil is the author of the deed."[103]

So magic, in its bad sense, is for Bacon either vain and illusory or diabolical – tricks or witchcraft. Quite distinct from all this are the powers employed by wise men when they make use of astral images, incantations, and so forth. These are natural. It is just that the extent of the unknown powers of nature is so enormous that the wise men usually keep them secret, in part to avoid the charge of magic. Perhaps it is this belief that got him locked up.

I hope I have in no way suggested that Roger Bacon was "typical". Throughout this book I have been exploring debates, alternative and competing theories, and differing views about the boundaries and the substance of the natural and the supernatural. Even in the narrow range of thought on which I have mainly concentrated, that is, the views committed to writing by educated men, there was great diversity. It would be false to take as typical either Manegold of Lautenbach's scriptural fundamentalism or Dante's naturalistic theorizing, to regard as representative either those who carved the dog-heads at Vézelay or the Franciscan missionaries who came to doubt their existence. So there was a range of opinion in the medieval period, of which Bacon's is one strand.

It is a strand with a strong individual coloration. There is no question that Bacon's character comes through in his writings more strongly than is the case with most writers of the thirteenth century. He emerges as a voluble, courageous, and deeply

---

[103] Et per cultellum possum scindere panem et hominem vulnerare. Sic similiter per verba potest sapiens sapienter operari, et magicus magice.... unus facit per potestatem naturalem; alius aut nihil facit, aut diabolus auctor est operis: *Opus tertium* 26, ed. Brewer, pp. 95–6; the knife analogy also in *Opus maius* 4, ed. Bridges 1, p. 394, tr. Burke, p. 410.

obsessive personality, ready to turn the conversation to the topic of mirrors or the Antichrist at any moment. One can imagine encountering him as a fellow traveller on a journey and finding him fascinating and interesting but being resolutely determined not to exchange addresses at the end of the voyage. He expressed a high regard for his own talents, in fields as diverse as optics, calendar reform, and foreign languages, perhaps, at least in the last case, overestimating his own abilities and underestimating those of others, particularly his contemporaries.[104] He saw himself in the line of Aristotle, Avicenna, and Averroes, and if asked the question "Who is there like us?" he would have replied "Precious few and they're all dead".

Yet his arrogance was, in all likelihood, a defensive response to his situation. He really was something of a pioneer with a vision rather unusual among his contemporaries. There were, of course, plenty of Scholastic thinkers who aspired to create general intellectual schemes that would cover the whole of the knowable universe. These schemes were, however, theological, in that they started from the premises of revealed truth and concentrated on the salvation story. Bonaventure, head of Bacon's order at the time he composed the *Opus maius*, provides a classic representative of this kind of systematic theology. On the other hand, the scholars of the thirteenth century writing on astronomy, medicine, and natural history did not usually integrate their

---

[104] Characteristic reservations are expressed in several of the essays in Little, *Roger Bacon: Essays* (as in note 3): "It would be idle to say that Bacon had arrived at any striking results in the study of comparative philology" (Hirsch, p. 103); "If we mean to inquire if he was justified, by his own wide knowledge of mathematics and by any great discoveries, in assuming the attitude of superiority which he showed towards most of his contemporaries, there can be but one answer, and that a negative one" (Smith, p. 182).

investigations into a Grand Theory. The shape of Bacon's Grand Theory is sometimes elusive. He wrote a lot, repeated himself often, and sometimes seems to have been confused even about the numbering of the parts of his great project.[105] Yet whether he succeeded or not, he aimed at producing an account of the universe in which there was a place both for certain fundamental explanatory physical principles, notably universal radiation, and also detailed empirical exposition of such things as the nerve system of the eye. What Pope Clement IV made of it all we do not know, but Bacon's work does leave the impression of a man with a bold and ambitious intellectual vision, namely, to produce an integrated scientific picture of the universe. Further, despite his recurrent arrogance of tone, there is even the occasional attractive note of humility as he contemplates the task. This is what he says about the fly: "No one is so wise concerning the natures of things that he can have certain knowledge of all the truths there are about the nature and properties of a single fly. He cannot tell you the causes of its colour, and why it has so many feet, and not more nor less, nor give a full account of its limbs and properties."[106] So even one fly exhausts the possibilities of

---

[105] A passage from Theodore Crowley, *Roger Bacon: The Problem of the Soul in His Philosophical Commentaries* (Louvain and Dublin, 1950), pp. 64–5, may be cited as an indication of the complexity of the situation: "the treatise *De Multiplicatione Specierum* edited by Bridges is part of a larger work ... Delorme has suggested that this larger work was part of the *Metaphysics* frequently referred to in the *Communia Naturalium*. Besides we know that Bacon wrote a special treatise, *Tractatus de Radiis*, for Clement IV. This is certainly not the treatise published by Bridges under the misleading title *De multiplicatione Specierum* which is but one part of a treatise that comprises at least four parts."

[106] Nam nullus est ita sapiens in rerum naturis qui sciret certificare de veritatibus omnibus quae sunt circa naturam et proprietates unius muscae, nec sciret dare causas proprias coloris ejus, et quare tot pedes nec plures nec

complete human knowledge of the natural world. Along with his febrile sensitivity to mirrors, his urgency about the task of instruction in mathematics and languages, and his bruised sense of self-esteem, Roger Bacon was also aware of the infinite variety, complexity, and ultimate mystery of Nature.

pauciores haberet, nec rationem reddere de membris et ejus proprietatibus: *Opus maius* 1. 10, ed. Bridges 3, p. 23, tr. Burke, p. 24; cf. *Opus maius* 7. 4. 2. 3, ed. Massa, p. 209, tr. Burke, p. 803.

Bibliography of Works Cited

PRIMARY SOURCES

Adam of Bremen, *Gesta Hammaburgensis ecclesiae pontificum*, ed. Werner Trillmich, *Quellen des 9. und 11. Jahrhunderts zur Geschichte der Hamburgischen Kirche und des Reiches* (Ausgewählte Quellen zur deutschen Geschichte des Mittelalters 11, Darmstadt, 1961), pp. 135–503.

Addison, Joseph, *The Drummer* (London, 1716).

Aethicus, *Cosmographia*, ed. Otto Prinz (Quellen zur Geistesgeschichte des Mittelalters 14, Munich, 1993).

Albertus Magnus, *Summa Theologica*, in his *Opera omnia* 32, ed. A. Borgnet (Paris, 1895).

Albumasar (Abu Ma'shar), *De magnis coniunctionibus*, ed. Keiji Yamamoto and Charles Burnett, *On Historical Astrology: The Book of Religions and Dynasties (On the Great Conjunctions)* (2 vols., Leiden, 2000).

Aldhelm, *De virginitate (Carmen)*, ed. Rudolf Ehwald, *Monumenta Germaniae Historica, Auctores antiquissimi* 15 (Berlin, 1919), pp. 350–471.

Alexander of Hales, *Summa theologica* (4 vols. in 5, plus index vol., Quarracchi, 1924–79).

Ambrose, *Hexaemeron*, ed. C. Schenkl (Corpus scriptorum ecclesiasticorum latinorum 32/1, Vienna, 1897).

Annals of Ulster 1, ed. Seán Mac Airt and Gearóid Mac Niocaill (Dublin, 1983).

Anselm, *Gesta episcoporum Leodensium*, ed. R. Köpke, *Monumenta Germaniae Historica, Scriptores* 7 (Hanover, 1846), pp. 189–234.

Aristotle, *Politicorum libri octo cum vetusta translatione Guilelmi de Moerbeka*, ed. F. Susemihl (Leipzig, 1872).

Attenborough, F. L., ed., *The Laws of the Earliest English Kings* (Cambridge, 1922).

Augustine, *De civitate dei*, ed. B. Dombart and A. Kalb (2 vols., Corpus Christianorum, series latina 47–8, 1955).

————, *De genesi ad litteram*, ed. J. Zycha (Corpus Scriptorum Ecclesiasticorum Latinorum 28, 1894).

Bacon, Francis, *Advancement of Learning* (London, 1605).

Bartholomaeus Anglicus, *De proprietatibus rerum* (Cologne, 1472, and many other printings).

Bernardus Silvestris, *Cosmographia*, ed. Peter Dronke (Leiden, 1978).

Bestiarium: die Texte der Handschrift MS. Ashmole 1511 der Bodleian Library Oxford in lateinischer und deutscher Sprache, ed. Franz Unterkircher (Interpretationes ad codices 3, Graz, 1986).

Bonaventure, *Legenda maior S. Francisci, Analecta Franciscana* 10 (1926–41), pp. 555–652.

Boniface, *Epistulae*, ed. Reinhold Rau (Ausgewählte Quellen zur deutschen Geschichte des Mittelalters 4b, Darmstadt, 1968).

————, *Sermo* 15, "De abrenuntiatione in baptismate", *Patrologia latina* 89, cols. 870–2.

Burchard of Worms, *Decretum, Patrologia latina* 140, cols. 537–1058.

Caesarius of Arles, *Sermones*, ed. Germain Morin (2 vols., Corpus Christianorum, series latina 103–4, 1953).

Caesarius of Heisterbach, *Dialogus miraculorum*, ed. J. Strange (2 vols. and index, Cologne, etc., 1851–7).

Capitula Rotomagensia, ed. Rudolf Pokorny, *Monumenta Germaniae Historica, Capitula Episcoporum* 3 (Hanover, 1995), pp. 367–71.

Capitulatio de partibus Saxonie, ed. Alfred Boretius, *Monumenta Germaniae Historica, Capitularia regum Francorum* 1 (Hanover, 1883), pp. 68–70, no. 26.

Cathwulf, *Epistola* 7, in *Epistolae variorum*, ed. Ernst Dümmler, *Monumenta Germaniae Historica, Epistolae 4 (Karolini aevi 2)* (Hanover, 1895), pp. 501–5.

Chartularium Universitatis Parisiensis 1 (1200–1286), ed. Henri Denifle (Paris, 1889).

Chronica XXIV Generalium Ordinis Minorum, Analecta Franciscana 3 (1897).

Comnena, Anna, *The Alexiad*, ed. B. Leib (3 vols., Paris, 1937–45); tr. E. R. A. Sewter (Penguin Classics, 1969).

Dante Alighieri, *Convivio: Testo*, ed. Franca Brambilla Ageno (*Opere di Dante* 3/2, Florence, 1995).

———, *De situ et forma aque et terre*, ed. Giorgio Padoan (*Opere di Dante* 8/3, Florence, 1968).

———, *Inferno*, in *La commedia secondo l'antica vulgata* 2, ed. Giorgio Petrocchi (*Opere di Dante* 7/2, reprint, Florence, 1994).

Dietrich von Apolda, *Vita S. Dominici, Acta Sanctorum*, Augusti 1 (Antwerp, 1733), pp. 562–632.

Dionysius the Areopagite (Pseudo) (Denys l'Aréopagite), *La Hiérarchie céleste*, ed. and tr. Günter Heil and Maurice de Gandillac (Sources chrétiennes 58, 1958).

Disraeli, Isaac, *Curiosities of Literature* (London, 1791, 5th ed., 2 vols., 1807).

Doyle, Arthur Conan, *The Lost World* (London and New York, 1912).

Edictus Rothari, ed. Friedrich Bluhme, *Edictus ceteraeque Langobardorum leges, Monumenta Germaniae Historica, Fontes Iuris Germanici Antiqui* 2 (Hanover, 1869), pp. 1–73.

The Famous Historie of Fryer Bacon (London, 1627).

Fernández de Navarette, M., ed., *Viajes de Colón* (Mexico, 1986).

Frederick II, *Constitutions of Melfi*, ed. Wolfgang Stürner, *Die Konstitutionen Friedrichs II. für das Königreich Sizilien, Monumenta Germaniae Historica, Constitutiones et acta publica imperatorum et regum* 2, suppl. (Hanover, 1996).

Fulcher of Chartres, *Historia Hierosolymitana*, ed. Heinrich Hagenmeyer (Heidelberg, 1913).

Gerald of Wales (Giraldus Cambrensis), *Descriptio Kambriae*, in his *Opera*, ed. J. S. Brewer, J. F. Dimock, and G. F. Warner (8 vols., Rerum Britannicarum Medii Aevi Scriptores, 1861–91) 6, pp. 153–227.

———, *Speculum Duorum*, ed. Yves Lefèvre, R. B. C. Huygens and Michael Richter (Cardiff, 1974).

Gervase of Tilbury, *Otia Imperialia*, ed. S. E. Banks and J. W. Binns (Oxford, 2002).

Gilbert Crispin, *Vita Herluini, Patrologia latina* 150, cols. 697–714; ed. Anna Sapir Abulafia and G. R. Evans, *The Works of Gilbert Crispin* (London, 1986), pp. 185–212.

Godefroy de Saint–Victor, *Microcosmus*, ed. Philippe Delhaye (Lille and Gembloux, 1951).

Gregory the Great, *Dialogi*, ed. Adalbert de Vogüé (Sources chrétiennes 251, 260, 265, 1978–80).

Haggard, H. Rider, *King Solomon's Mines* (London, 1885).

Henry of Livonia, *Chronicon Livoniae*, ed. Leonid Arbusow and Albert Bauer, *Monumenta Germaniae Historica, Scriptores rerum germanicarum in usum scholarum* 31 (Hanover, 1955) and *Ausgewählte Quellen zur deutschen Geschichte des Mittelalters* 24 (Darmstadt, 1959).

Hergé, *Le Temple du Soleil* (Paris, 1949); Eng. tr., *The Adventures of Tintin: Prisoners of the Sun* (London, 1962).

Hilton, James, *Lost Horizon* (London, 1933).

Das Homiliar des Bischofs von Prag, ed. F. Hecht (Beiträge zur Geschichte Böhmens, Abt. 1, 1, Prague, 1863).

Hostiensis (Henry de Segusio), *Summa aurea* (Lyons, 1548).

Hrabanus Maurus, *De computo*, ed. Wesley M. Stevens (Corpus Christianorum, continuatio medievalis 44, 1979).

———, *Epistolae*, ed. Ernst Dümmler, *Monumenta Germaniae Historica, Epistolae 5 (Karolini aevi 3)* (Berlin, 1899), pp. 379–516.

———, *Homilia* 42: "Contra eos qui in lunae defectu clamoribus se fatigabant", in *Patrologia latina* 110, cols. 78–80 (see also Woods in Secondary Works).

Indiculus superstitionum, ed. Alfred Boretius, *Monumenta Germaniae Historica, Capitularia regum Francorum* 1 (Hanover, 1883), pp. 222–3, no. 108; ed. Reinhold Rau, in *Boniface, Epistulae* (Ausgewählte Quellen zur deutschen Geschichte des Mittelalters 4b, Darmstadt, 1968), pp. 444–8.

Inquisitio de fide, vita et moribus, fama et miraculis ... Thome de Cantilupo (MS Vatican City, Biblioteca Apostolica Vaticana, Vat. Lat. 4015).

Isidore of Seville, *Etymologiae*, ed. W. M. Lindsay (2 vols., Oxford, 1911, unpaginated).

———, *Étymologies Livre XII: Des animaux*, ed. Jacques André (Paris, 1986).

Jocelin of Furness, *Vita Patricii, Acta sanctorum*, Martii 2 (Antwerp, 1668), pp. 540–80.

John Beleth, *Summa de ecclesiasticis officiis*, ed. Heribert Douteil (2 vols., Corpus Christianorum, continuatio medievalis 41–41A, 1976).

John de Marignollis, *Chronicon Bohemorum*, ed. J. Emler, *Fontes Rerum Bohemicarum* 3 (Prague, 1882), pp. 492–604; extracts in *Sinica Franciscana I: Itinera et Relationes fratrum minorum saec. XIII et XIV*, ed. Anastasius van den Wyngaert (Quaracchi, 1929), pp. 524–60, and, in translation, in *Cathay and the Way Thither* 3, ed. Henry Yule (2nd ed., rev. Henri Cordier, Hakluyt Society, 2nd Ser., 37, 1914), pp. 175–269.

John de Sacrobosco, *Tractatus de spera*, ed. Lynn Thorndike, *'The Sphere' of Sacrobosco and Its Commentators* (Chicago, 1949).

John of Salisbury, *Metalogicon*, ed. J. B. Hall and K. S. B. Keats-Rohan (Corpus Christianorum, continuatio medievalis 98, 1991).

John the Scot Eriugena, *Periphyseon*, ed. Edouard Jeaneau (5 vols., Corpus Christianorum, continuatio medievalis 161–5, 1996–2003).

Kindi, al-, *De Radiis*, ed. M.-Th. D'Alverny and F. Hudry, *Archives d'histoire doctrinale et littéraire du moyen âge* 41 (1974), pp. 139–260.

The Laws of the Medieval Kingdom of Hungary 1, ed. Janos M. Bak et al. (Bakersfield, CA, 1989).

Lex Salica, ed. Karl August Eckhardt, *Monumenta Germaniae Historica, Leges nationum Germanicarum* 4/2 (Hanover, 1969).

Macrobius, *In Somnium Scipionis*, ed. Mireille Armisen-Marchetti (2 vols., Paris, 2003).

Manegold of Lautenbach, *Liber contra Wolfelmum*, ed. Wilfried Hartmann, *Monumenta Germaniae Historica, Quellen zur Geistesgeschichte des Mittelalters* 8 (Weimar, 1972).

Maximus of Turin, *Sermones*, ed. Almut Mutzenbecher (Corpus Christianorum, series latina 23, 1962).

Memoirs of the Extraordinary Life, Works, and Discoveries of Martinus Scriblerus, ed. Charles Kerby-Miller (New Haven, 1950).

More, Henry, *The Immortality of the Soul* (London, 1659).

Newton, Isaac, *Theological Manuscripts*, ed. Herbert McLachlan (Liverpool, 1950).

Odo of Deuil, *De profectione Ludovici VII in Orientem*, ed. Virginia G. Berry (New York, 1948).

Oliver of Paderborn (or Cologne), *Historia damiatina*, ed. Hermann Hoogeweg, *Die Schriften des Kölner Domscholasters...Oliverus* (Bibliothek des literarischen Vereins in Stuttgart 202, Tübingen, 1894), pp. 159–282.

Pactus legis Salicae, ed. Karl August Eckhardt, *Monumenta Germaniae Historica, Leges nationum Germanicarum* 4/1 (Hanover, 1962).

"The Passion of St Christopher", ed. and tr. J. Fraser, *Revue Celtique* 34 (1913), pp. 307–25.

Peter Lombard, *Sententiae in IV libris distinctae*, ed. Collegium S. Bonaventurae (3rd ed., 2 vols., *Spicilegium Bonaventurianum* 4–5, Grottaferrata, 1971–81).

Peter of Cornwall, *Liber revelationum* (Lambeth Palace MS 51).

Peter of Zittau, *Chronicon Aule Regie*, ed. J. Emler, *Fontes Rerum Bohemicarum* 4 (Prague, 1884), pp. 1–337.

Peter the Chanter, *Verbum abbreviatum, Patrologia latina* 205, cols. 23–270.

Piché, David, and Claude Lafleur, *La Condemnation parisienne de 1277* (Paris, 1999) (edition and discussion).

Pliny, *Historia naturalis*, ed. H. Rackham et al. (10 vols., Cambridge, MA, 1938–62).

Processus de Vita et Miraculis B. Petri de Luxemburgo, Acta sanctorum, Julii 1 (Antwerp, 1719), pp. 527–607.

Ratramnus of Corbie, *Epistola 12*, in *Epistolae Variorum*, ed. Ernst Dümmler, *Monumenta Germaniae Historica, Epistolae 6 (Karolini aevi 4)* (Berlin, 1925), pp. 155–7.

Regino of Prüm, *Libri duo de synodalibus causis et disciplinis ecclesiasticis*, ed. Wilfried Hartmann (Darmstadt, 2004).

Reiner, *Vita Evracli*, ed. Wilhelm Arndt, *Monumenta Germaniae Historica, Scriptores* 20 (Hanover, 1868), pp. 561–5.

Robertson, A. J., ed., *Laws of the Kings of England from Edmund to Henry I* (Cambridge, 1925).

Rodulfus Glaber, *Historiarum libri quinque*, in his *Opera*, ed. John France (Oxford, 1989).

Roger Bacon, *Compendium studii philosophiae*, ed. J. S. Brewer, *Fr. Rogeri Bacon opera quaedam hactenus inedita* 1 (Rerum Britannicarum Medii Aevi Scriptores, 1859), pp. 393–519.

————, *Compendium studii theologiae*, ed. H. Rashdall (British Society of Franciscan Studies 3, 1911); ed. and tr. Thomas S. Maloney (Leiden, 1988).

————, *De multiplicatione specierum*, ed. David C. Lindberg, *Roger Bacon's Philosophy of Nature* (Oxford, 1983), pp. 1–269.

————, *Moralis philosophia*, ed. Eugenio Massa (Zurich, 1953).

————, *Opera hactenus inedita Rogeri Baconis*, ed. Robert Steele and Ferdinand M. Delorme (16 vols., Oxford, 1905–40).

————, *Opus maius*, ed. J. H. Bridges (3 vols., London, 1900).

————, *The Opus Majus of Roger Bacon*, tr. Robert Belle Burke (2 vols., Philadelphia, 1928, paginated continuously).

————, *Opus minus*, ed. J. S. Brewer, *Fr. Rogeri Bacon opera quaedam hactenus inedita* 1 (Rerum Britannicarum Medii Aevi Scriptores, 1859), pp. 313–89.

————, *Opus tertium*, ed. J. S. Brewer, ibid., pp. 1–310.

————, *Part of the 'Opus tertium' of Roger Bacon*, ed. A. G. Little (Aberdeen, 1912).

————, *Roger Bacon's Philosophy of Nature*, ed. David C. Lindberg (Oxford, 1983).

————, *Un Fragment inédit de L'Opus tertium*, ed. Pierre Duhem (Quaracchi, 1909).

————, "An Unedited Part of Roger Bacon's *Opus maius*: De signis", ed. K. M. Fredborg, L. Nielsen, and J. Pinborg, *Traditio* 34 (1978), pp. 75–136.

————, "An Unpublished Fragment of a Work by Roger Bacon", ed. F. L. Gasquet, *English Historical Review* 12 (1897), pp. 494–517.

————, see also *Secretum secretorum*.

Roger Bacon (attrib.), *Epistola de secretis operibus artis naturae et de nullitate magiae*, ed. J. S. Brewer, *Fr. Rogeri Bacon opera quaedam hactenus inedita* 1 (Rerum Britannicarum Medii Aevi Scriptores, 1859), pp. 523–51.

Saxo Grammaticus, *Gesta Danorum*, ed. J. Olrik and H. Raeder (2 vols., Copenhagen, 1931–57).

Secretum secretorum, ed. Robert Steele (Opera hactenus inedita Rogeri Baconi 5, Oxford, 1920).

Stephen de Bourbon, *Tractatus de diversis materiis praedicabilibus*, ed. A. Lecoy de la Marche, *Anecdotes historiques, légendes et apologues tirés du receuil inédit d'Etienne de Bourbon* (Société de l'Histoire de la France 185, 1877).

Thietmar of Merseburg, *Chronicon*, ed. Robert Holtzmann, *Monumenta Germaniae Historica, Scriptores rerum germanicarum*, new series 9 (Berlin, 1935); ed. Werner Trillmich (Ausgewählte Quellen zur deutschen Geschichte des Mittelalters 9, Darmstadt, 1957).

Thomas à Kempis, *The Earliest English Translation of the First Three Books of the De imitatione Christi*, ed. John K. Ingram (Early English Text Society, extra series 63, 1893).

Thomas Aquinas, *Opera omnia*, ed. Roberto Busa (7 vols., Stuttgart-Bad Cannstatt, 1980).

Vita Eligii episcopi Noviomagensis, ed. Bruno Krusch, *Monumenta Germaniae Historica, Scriptores rerum Merovingicarum* 4 (Hanover and Leipzig, 1902), pp. 663–741.

Vita Norberti, ed. Roger Wilmans, *Monumenta Germaniae Historica, Scriptores* 12 (Hanover, 1856), pp. 670–703; ed. Hatto Kallfelz, *Lebensbeschreibungen einiger Bischöfe des 10.–12. Jahrhunderts* (Ausgewählte Quellen zur deutschen Geschichte des Mittelalters 22, Darmstadt, 1973), pp. 452–540.

Wasserschleben, F. W. H., ed., *Die Bussordnungen der abendländischen Kirche* (Halle, 1851).

Westrem, Scott D., ed., *The Hereford Map: A Transcription and Translation of the Legends with Commentary* (Terrarum Orbis 1, Turnhout, 2001).

William de Tocco, *Vita S. Thomae Aquinatis, Fontes Vitae S. Thomas Aquinatis*, ed. D. Prümmer and M.-H. Laurent (Documents inédits publiés par la Revue Thomiste, 6 fascicules, 1912–37), pp. 57–160 (fasc. 2); ed. Claire Le Brun-Gouanvic, *Ystoria sancti Thome de Aquino de Guillaume de Tocco (1323). Édition critique, introduction et notes* (Studies and Texts 127: Pontifical Institute of Medieval Studies, Toronto, 1996).

William of Auvergne, *De legibus*, in his *Opera omnia* (2 vols., Orleans, 1674, reprint Frankfurt, 1963) 1, pp. 18–102.

——, *De universo*, ibid., pp. 593–1074.

——, *The Universe of Creatures*, tr. Roland J. Teske (Milwaukee, 1998).

William of Moerbeke, *see Aristotle*.

William of Newburgh, *Historia rerum anglicarum*, ed. Richard Howlett, *Chronicles of the Reigns of Stephen, Henry II and Richard I* (4 vols., Rerum Britannicarum Medii Aevi Scriptores, 1884–9) 1–2.

William of Rubruck, *Itinerarium*, ed. Anastasius van den Wyngaert, *Sinica Franciscana I: Itinera et Relationes fratrum minorum saec. XIII et XIV* (Quaracchi, 1929), pp. 164–332; in translation as "The Journey of William of Rubruck", in *The Mongol Mission*, ed. Christopher Dawson (London, 1955, repr. as *Mission to Asia*, Toronto, 1980), pp. 87–220, and in *The Mission of Friar William of Rubruck*, ed. Peter Jackson and David Morgan (Hakluyt Society, 2nd Ser., 173, 1990).

SECONDARY LITERATURE

Alessio, F., "Un secolo di studi su Ruggero Bacon (1848–1957)", *Rivista critica di storia della filosofia* 14 (1959), pp. 81–102.

Bartlett, Robert, *The Hanged Man: A Story of Miracle, Memory and Colonization in the Middle Ages* (Princeton, 2004).

Berceville, Gilles, "L'Étonnante alliance: évangile et miracles selon saint Thomas d'Aquin", *Revue Thomiste* 103 (2003), pp. 5–74.

Berschin, Walther, *Greek Letters and the Latin Middle Ages* (Eng. tr., Washington, DC, 1988).

Bertrand, Olivier, "Les Néologismes religieux dans la traduction de la Cité de Dieu par Raoul de Presles ou comment christianiser le lexique latin", in *Actes du 23e Congrès International de Linguistique et de Philologie Romanes*, ed. Fernando Sanchez Miret (6 vols. in 5, Tübingen, 2003) 3, pp. 43–7.

Biernoff, Suzannah, *Sight and Embodiment in the Middle Ages* (Basingstoke, 2002).

Boffito, Giuseppe, "Intorno alla "Quaestio de aqua et terra" attribuita a Dante I: la controversia dell'acqua e della terra prima e dopo di Dante", *Memorie della Reale Accademia delle Scienze di Torino*, 2nd ser., 51 (1902), pp. 73–159.

Broedel, Hans Peter, *The Malleus Maleficarum and the Construction of Witchcraft* (Manchester, 2003).

Bromwich, Rachel, A. O. H. Jarman, and Brynley F. Roberts, eds., *The Arthur of the Welsh: The Arthurian Legend in Medieval Welsh Literature* (Cardiff, 1991).

Brown, Peter, "Society and the Supernatural: A Medieval Change", *Daedalus* 104 (1975), pp. 133–51 (repr. in his *Society and the Holy in Late Antiquity* (Berkeley and Los Angeles, 1982), pp. 302–32).

Bruce, Scott G., "Hagiography as Monstrous Ethnography: A Note on Ratramnus of Corbie's Letter Concerning the Conversion of the Cynocephali", in *Insignis Sophiae Arcator: Medieval Latin Studies in Honour of Michael Herren on his 65th Birthday*, ed. G. Wieland, C. Ruff and R. G. Arthur (Turnhout, 2006), pp. 45–56.

Buckler, Georgina, *Anna Comnena: A Study* (Oxford, 1929).

Burnett, Charles, "The Introduction of Aristotle's Natural Philosophy into Great Britain: A Preliminary Survey of the Manuscript Evidence", in *Aristotle in Britain during the Middle Ages*, ed. John Marenbon (Turnhout, 1996), pp. 21–50.

Bynum, Caroline Walker, *Metamorphosis and Identity* (New York, 2001).

———, "Miracles and Marvels: The Limits of Alterity", in *Vita religiosa im Mittelalter: Festschrift für Kaspar Elm zum 70. Geburtstag*, ed. Franz J. Felten and Nikolas Jaspert (Berlin, 1999), pp. 799–817.

Chiffoleau, Jacques, "*Contra Naturam*: pour une approche casuistique et procédurale de la nature médiévale", *Micrologus* 4 (1996), pp. 265–312.

Clark, Stuart, *Thinking with Demons: The Idea of Witchcraft in Early Modern Europe* (Oxford, 1997).

Clegg, Brian, *The First Scientist: A Life of Roger Bacon* (London, 2003).

Crowley, Theodore, *Roger Bacon: The Problem of the Soul in His Philosophical Commentaries* (Louvain and Dublin, 1950).

d'Alverny, Marie-Thérèse, "Translations and Translators", in *Renaissance and Renewal in the Twelfth Century*, ed. Robert Benson and Giles Constable (Cambridge, MA, and Oxford, 1982), pp. 421–62.

d'Occhieppo, Konradin Ferrari, "Zur Identifizierung der Sonnenfinsternis während des Petschenegenkrieges Alexios' I. Komnenos (1084)", *Jahrbuch der österreichischen Byzantinistik* (1974), pp. 179–84.

Dall'Olmo, Umberto, "*Eclypsis naturalis* ed *eclypsis prodigialis* nelle cronache medioevali", *Organon* 15 (1979), pp. 153–66.

Daston, Lorraine, "Marvelous Facts and Miraculous Evidence in Early Modern Europe", *Critical Inquiry* 18 (1991), pp. 93–124.

Davies, Rees, *Domination and Conquest: The Experience of Ireland, Scotland and Wales 1100–1300* (Cambridge, 1990).

Delhaye, Philippe, *Le Microcosmus de Godefroy de Saint-Victor: étude théologique* (Lille and Gembloux, 1951).

Der Nersessian, Sirarpie, *Miniature Painting in the Armenian Kingdom of Cilicia from the Twelfth to the Fourteenth Century* (Dumbarton Oaks Studies 31, 2 vols., 1993).

Dickey, James, *The Whole Motion: Collected Poems 1945–1992* (Hanover, NH, 1992).

Dictionary of Medieval Latin from British Sources (Oxford University Press for the British Academy, 1975–).

Dictionnaire historique de la langue française, ed. Alain Rey (2 vols., Paris, 1992).

Dijksterhuis, Eduard Jan, *De mechanisering van het Wereldbeeld* (Amsterdam, 1950); Eng tr., *The Mechanization of the World Picture* (Oxford, 1961).

Draelants, Isabelle, "Le Temps dans les textes historiographiques du Moyen Âge", in *Le Temps qu'il fait au Moyen Âge: phénomènes atmosphériques dans la littérature, la pensée scientifique et religieuse*, ed. Joëlle Ducos and Claude Thomasset (Paris, 1998), pp. 91–138.

Fanger, Claire, "Things Done Wisely by a Wise Enchanter: Negotiating the Power of Words in the Thirteenth Century", *Esoterica* 1 (1999), pp. 97–132.

Friedman, John B., *The Monstrous Races in Medieval Art and Thought* (Cambridge, MA, 1981, reprint Syracuse, 2000).

Garrison, Mary, "Letters to a King and Biblical *exempla*: The Examples of Cathuulf and Clemens Peregrinus", *Early Medieval Europe* 7 (1998), pp. 305–28.

Gutas, Dimitri, *Greek Thought, Arabic Culture: The Graeco-Arabic Translation Movement in Baghdad and Early 'Abbasid Society* (London, 1998).

Hackett, Jeremiah, "Roger Bacon", in *A Companion to Philosophy in the Middle Ages*, ed. Jorge J. E. Gracia and Timothy B. Noone (Malden, MA, and Oxford, 2003), pp. 616–25.

———, ed., *Roger Bacon and the Sciences: Commemorative Essays* (Studien und Texte zur Geistesgeschichte des Mittelalters 57, Leiden, 1997).

———, "Roger Bacon on *Scientia Experimentalis*", ibid., pp. 277–315.

Hackett, Jeremiah, and Thomas S. Maloney, "A Roger Bacon Bibliography (1957–1985)", *New Scholasticism* 61 (1987), pp. 184–207.

Hamesse, Jacqueline, "*Experientia/experimentum* dans les lexiques médiévaux et dans les textes philosophiques antérieurs au 14e siècle", in *Experientia: Colloquio Internazionale del Lessico Intellettuale Europeo*, ed. M. Veneziani (Florence, 2002), pp. 77–90.

Hamilton, Bernard, "'God Wills It': Signs of Divine Approval in the Crusade Movement", in *Signs, Wonders, Miracles: Representations of Divine Power in the Life of the Church*, ed. Kate Cooper and Jeremy Gregory (Studies in Church History 41, 2005), pp. 88–98.

Hardon, John A., "The Concept of Miracle from St. Augustine to Modern Apologetics", *Theological Studies* 15 (1954), pp. 229–57.

Harmening, Dieter, *Superstitio: Überlieferungs- und theoriengeschichtliche Untersuchungen zur kirchlich-theologischen Aberglaubensliteratur des Mittelalters* (Berlin, 1979).

Harvey, E. Ruth, *The Inward Wits: Psychological Theory in the Middle Ages and the Renaissance* (Warburg Institute Surveys 6, London, 1975).

Heck, Erich, *Roger Bacon: Ein mittelalterlicher Versuch einer historischen und systematischen Religionswissenschaft* (Bonn, 1957).

Heidemann, Joseph, *Papst Clemens IV: Das Vorleben des Papstes und sein Legationsregister* (Kirchengeschichtliche Studien 6/4, Münster, 1903).

Kieckhefer, Richard, *Unquiet Souls: Fourteenth-Century Saints and Their Religious Milieu* (Chicago, 1984).

Kretzmann, Norman, Anthony Kenny, and Jan Pinborg, eds., *The Cambridge History of Later Medieval Philosophy* (Cambridge, 1982).

Kuhn, Thomas, *The Structure of Scientific Revolutions* (Chicago, 1962).

Le Goff, Jacques, "The Marvelous in the Medieval West", in *The Medieval Imagination* (Eng. tr., Chicago, 1988), pp. 27–44.

Lea, Henry Charles, *A History of the Inquisition of the Middle Ages* (3 vols., New York, 1888).

———, *Materials toward a History of Witchcraft* (3 vols., Philadelphia, 1939).

Lemay, Richard, "Roger Bacon's Attitude toward the Latin Translations and Translators of the Twelfth and Thirteenth Centuries", in *Roger Bacon and the Sciences: Commemorative Essays*, ed. Jeremiah Hackett (Studien und Texte zur Geistesgeschichte des Mittelalters 57, Leiden, 1997), pp. 25–47.

Lewis, C. S., "On Science Fiction", in *Of Other Worlds* (London, 1966), pp. 59–73.

————, *Studies in Words* (Cambridge, 1960).

Lexicon der christliche Ikonographie, ed. Wolfgang Braunfels (8 vols., Rome, etc., 1968–76).

Ley, Klaus, "Dante als Wissenschaftler: die 'Quaestio de aqua et terra'", *Deutsches Dantes Jahrbuch* 58 (1983), pp. 41–71.

Lindberg, David C., ed., *Science in the Middle Ages* (Chicago, 1978).

Lionarons, Joyce Tally, "From Monster to Martyr: The Old English Legend of Saint Christopher", in *Marvels, Monsters, and Miracles: Studies in the Medieval and Early Modern Imaginations*, ed. Timothy S. Jones and David A. Sprunger (Kalamazoo, 2002), pp. 167–82.

Little, A. G., ed., *Roger Bacon: Essays Contributed by Various Writers on the Occasion of the Commemoration of the Seventh Centenary of His Birth* (Oxford, 1914).

Lubac, Henri de, *Surnaturel: études historiques* (Paris, 1946).

Luscombe, David, "The State of Nature and the Origin of the State", in *The Cambridge History of Later Medieval Philosophy*, ed. Norman Kretzmann, Anthony Kenny, and Jan Pinborg (Cambridge, 1982), pp. 757–70.

————, "Roger Bacon and Language", in *Britannia latina: Latin in the Culture of Great Britain from the Middle Ages to the Twentieth Century*, ed. Charles Burnett and Nicholas Mann (Warburg Institute Colloquia 8, 2005), pp. 42–54.

Maddicott, John, *Simon de Montfort* (Cambridge, 1994).

Maloney, Thomas S., "A Roger Bacon Bibliography (1985–1995)", in *Roger Bacon and the Sciences: Commemorative Essays*, ed. Jeremiah Hackett (Studien und Texte zur Geistesgeschichte des Mittelalters 57, Leiden, 1997), pp. 395–403.

Marrone, Steven B., "William of Auvergne on Magic in Natural Philosophy and Theology", in *Was ist Philosophie im Mittelalter?*, ed.

Jan Aertsen and Andreas Speer (Miscellanea Medievalia 26, Berlin, 1998), pp. 741–8.

McCarthy, Daniel, and Aidan Breen, "Astronomical Observations in the Irish Annals and their Motivation", *Peritia: Journal of the Medieval Academy of Ireland* 11 (1997), pp. 1–43.

Michaud-Quantin, Pierre, *Etudes sur le vocabulaire philosophique de Moyen Age* (Rome, 1970).

Molland, George, "Roger Bacon as Magician", *Traditio* 30 (1974), pp. 445–60.

———, "Bacon, Roger (c.1214–1292?)", in *Oxford Dictionary of National Biography* (Oxford, 2004) 3, pp. 176–81.

Nearing, Homer, Jr., "The Legend of Julius Caesar's British Conquest", *Proceedings of the Modern Language Association of America* 64 (1949), pp. 889–929.

Norlind, Arnold, *Das Problem des gegenseitigen Verhältnisses von Land und Wasser und seine Behandlung im Mittelalter* (Lund, 1918).

Norton, Leonard Jonathan, *Crusaders of Chemistry: Six Makers of the Modern World* (Garden City, NY, 1930).

A Patristic Greek Lexicon. ed. G. W. H. Lampe (Oxford, 1961).

Pedersen, Olaf, "Sacrobosco, John de (d. c.1236)", *Oxford Dictionary of National Biography* (Oxford, 2004) 48, pp. 549–50.

Pouliot, François, *La Doctrine du miracle chez Thomas d'Aquin: Deus in omnibus intime operatur* (Paris, 2005).

Power, Amanda, "A Mirror for Every Age: The Reputation of Roger Bacon", *English Historical Review* 121 (2006), pp. 657–92.

———, "The Views of Roger Bacon on Geography, World Religions and the Defence of Christendom as expressed in His *Opus maius*" (unpublished Ph.D., Cambridge University, 2003).

Quentin, Albrecht, *Naturkenntnisse und Naturanschauungen bei Wilhelm von Auvergne* (Hildesheim, 1976).

Radic, Radivoj, "George Pachymeres and Roger Bacon on the Comet from 1264", in *Srednovekovna khristiianska Evropa: iztok i zapad/Medieval Christian Europe: East and West*, ed. Vasil Gyuzelev and Anisava Miltenova (Sofia, 2002), pp. 485–9.

Reeves, Marjorie, *The Influence of Prophecy in the Later Middle Ages: A Study in Joachimism* (Oxford, 1969).

Rodinson, Maxime, "La Lune chez les Arabes et dans l'Islam", in *La Lune: mythes et rites* (Paris, 1962), pp. 151–215.

Rosier, Irène, *La Parole comme acte: sur la grammaire et la sémantique au XIIIe siècle* (Paris, 1994).

Rothmann, Michael, "*Mirabilia vero dicimus, quae nostrae cognitioni non subiacent, etiam cum sint naturalia.* Wundergeschichten zwischen Wissen und Unterhaltung: der 'Liber de mirabilibus mundi' ('Otia Imperialia') des Gervasius von Tilbury", in *Mirakel im Mittelalter: Konzeptionen, Erscheinungsformen, Deutungen*, ed. Martin Heinzelmann, Klaus Herbers and Dieter R. Bauer (Beiträge zur Hagiographie 3, Stuttgart, 2002), pp. 399–432.

Rouchon Mouilleron, Véronique, *Vézelay: The Great Romanesque Church* (Eng. tr., New York, 1999).

Russell, Jeffrey Burton, *Witchcraft in the Middle Ages* (Ithaca, 1972).

Santi, Francesco, "*Utrum Plantae et Bruta Animalia et Corpora Mineralia Remaneant post Finem Mundi*: l'animale eterno", *Micrologus* 4 (1996), pp. 231–64.

Sawyer, Birgit, *The Viking-Age Rune-Stones* (Oxford, 2000).

Schove, D. Justin, *Chronology of Eclipses and Comets AD 1–1000* (Woodbridge, 1984).

Sidelko, Paul L., "The Condemnation of Roger Bacon", *Journal of Medieval History* 22 (1996), pp. 69–81.

Smoller, Laura, "Defining the Boundaries of the Natural in Fifteenth-Century Brittany: The Inquest into the Miracles of Saint Vincent Ferrer (d. 1419)", *Viator* 28 (1997), pp. 333–59.

Southern, Richard W., *The Making of the Middle Ages* (London and New Haven, CT, 1953).

Story, Joanna, "Cathwulf, Kingship, and the Royal Abbey of Saint-Denis", *Speculum* (1999), pp. 1–21.

Swinburne, Richard, *The Concept of Miracle* (London, 1970).

Teske, Roland J., "William of Auvergne", in *A Companion to Philosophy in the Middle Ages*, ed. Jorge J. E. Gracia and Timothy B. Noone (Malden, MA, and Oxford, 2003), pp. 680–7.

Thorndike, Lynn, *A History of Magic and Experimental Science during the first Thirteen Centuries of Our Era* (2 vols., New York, 1923).

Tschacher, Werner, "Der Flug durch die Luft zwischen Illusionstheorie und Realitätsbeweis: Studien zum sogennanten Kanon Episcopi und zum Hexenflug", *Zeitschrift für Rechtsgeschichte, Kanonistische Abteilung* 85 (1999), pp. 225–76.

Van Hove, Aloïs, *La Doctrine du miracle chez saint Thomas et son accord avec les principes de la recherche scientifique* (Wetteren, 1927).

Van Moolenbroek, J., "Signs in the Heavens in Groningen and Friesland in 1214: Oliver of Cologne and Crusade Propaganda", *Journal of Medieval History* 13 (1987), pp. 251–72.

Vauchez, André, *Sainthood in the Late Middle Ages* (Eng. tr., Cambridge, 1997).

———, *Saints, prophètes et visionnaires: le pouvoir surnaturel au Moyen Âge* (Paris, 1999).

Ward, Benedicta, *Miracles and the Medieval Mind: Theory, Record and Event 1000–1215* (Aldershot and Philadelphia, 1982).

Weber, Max, *Wissenschaft als Beruf* (Stuttgart, 1995, originally published Munich and Leipzig, 1919).

Weill-Parot, Nicholas, *Les Images astrologiques au Moyen Age et à la Renaissance* (Paris, 2002).

White, Michael, *Isaac Newton: The Last Sorcerer* (London, 1997).

Willard, Charity Cannon, "Raoul de Presles's Translation of Saint Augustine's *De Civitate Dei*", in *Medieval Translators and their Craft*, ed. Jeanette Beer (Kalamazoo, 1989), pp. 329–46.

Williams, David, *Deformed Discourse: The Function of the Monster in Mediaeval Thought and Literature* (Montreal, 1996).

Wittkower, Rudolf, "Marvels of the East: A Study in the History of Monsters", in *Allegory and the Migration of Symbols* (London, 1977), pp. 45–74.

Wolfson, Harry A., "The Internal Senses in Latin, Arabic and Hebrew Philosophic Texts", *Harvard Theological Review* 28 (1935), pp. 69–133.

Wood, Ian, "Christians and Pagans in Ninth-century Scandinavia", in *The Christianization of Scandinavia*, ed. Birgit Sawyer, Peter Sawyer, and Ian Wood (Alingsås, 1987), pp. 36–67.

Woods, Jennifer Clare, "A Critical Edition of Sermons 42–64 from the ninth-century Latin Sermon Collection compiled by Hrabanus Maurus for Archbishop Haistulf of Mainz" (unpublished Ph.D., University of London, 1997).

Index

CPSIA information can be obtained at www.ICGtesting.com
Printed in the USA
LVOW07s0349310716

498394LV00005B/13/P